KT-239-912

CityPack
Brussels
& Bruges

**ANTHONY SATTIN &
SYLVIE FRANQUET**

*Anthony Sattin is the author of
several books and is a regular
contributor to the* Daily
Telegraph *and* The Sunday
Times. *Sylvie Franquet is a
linguist, has worked as a
model, translator and tour
manager, and writes a column
for the Belgian newspaper* De
Morgen. *Together they wrote
the AA Explorer Guides to*
Egypt *and the* Greek Islands.

Bruges centre
map shown
on inside back
cover

AA Publishing

Contents

About this book

KEY TO SYMBOLS

✚	map reference on the fold-out map accompanying this book (see below)	🚌	nearest bus or tram route
✉	address	🚢	nearest riverboat or ferry stop
☎	telephone number	♿	facilities for visitors with disabilities
🕐	opening times	✋	admission charge
🍴	restaurant or café on premises or nearby	↔	other nearby places of interest
🚇	nearest underground or Metro train station	❓	tours, lectures, or special events
🚆	nearest overground train station	➤	indicates the page where you will find a fuller description
		ℹ	tourist information

CityPack Brussels & Bruges is divided into six sections to cover the six most important aspects of your visit to Brussels and Bruges. It includes:

- The authors' view of the cities and their people
- Itineraries, walks and excursions
- The top 25 sights to visit – as selected by the authors
- Features about different aspects of the cities that make them special
- Detailed listings of restaurants, hotels, shops and nightlife
- Practical information

In addition, easy-to-read side panels provide fascinating extra facts and snippets, highlights of places to visit and invaluable practical advice.

CROSS-REFERENCES

To help you make the most of your visit, cross-references, indicated by ➤ , show you where to find additional information about a place or subject.

MAPS

- **The fold-out map** in the wallet at the back of the book has a comprehensive street plan of Brussels with an inset of Bruges city centre. All the map references given in the book refer to this map. For example, the Hôtel de Ville in the Grand'Place in Brussels has the following information: ✚ E7 indicating the grid square of the map in which the Hôtel de Ville will be found.
- **The city-centre maps** found on the inside front (Brussels) and back (Bruges) covers of the book itself are for quick reference. They show the Top 25 Sights in the two cities, described on pages 24–48, which are clearly plotted by number (❶ – ㉕, not page number) from west to east in each city.

PRICES

Where appropriate, an indication of the cost of an establishment is given by **£** signs: **£££** denotes higher prices, **££** denotes average prices, while **£** denotes lower charges.

BROUWER'J

BRUSSELS
& BRUGES
life

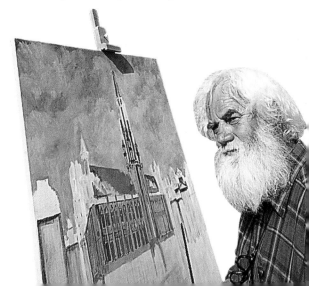

A PERSONAL VIEW

The Grand'Place in Brussels carpeted with flowers, a display created every other year

Brussels has one of the most unfortunate images of any Western capital. It is seen as a grey place from where European Community bureaucrats issue silly directives. But when you get to know the city better, you see that behind this façade lies a culture as rich and varied as its history. At heart it is a city of traders who have always placed a high value on the arts. As a result, in its architecture, its visual arts and its performances of music, theatre and dance, Brussels has enough to offer to keep you busy for this visit and your next.

Visitors who remember Brussels from 30 or 40 years ago are often shocked by the change, for its elegant centre has been transformed by great wealth (much of it institutional) and by what seems just as great neglect and bad planning on the part of the city council. The two most obvious reasons for this say a lot about the city, for while there has been an influx of bureaucrats to the international agencies (European Union, NATO, etc), many of the native Bruxellois have chosen to move out of the centre with its inner-city problems to green countryside, better schools and lower local taxes. This has left the

A great king

Although Belgium is a democracy, led by a prime minister, King Baudouin I, who died in 1993, did much to unify the country. He made a stand on matters where his principles were at stake: during the 1990 abortion debate, he found himself unable to sign the law, so abdicated for a day to allow it to be passed.

centre to the rich, supported by big business and international agencies, and to the poor, supported by the State.

Brussels can be a hard city to get to know, especially since its historic and obvious centre, the Grand'Place, is given over to tourists. Happily, it is a great place to walk around, with many of the sites in this guide close together. On the way you will find that, rather than being grey, Brussels is the colour

Bruges , a city of canals

of stone, of the green of its many parks and of the bright technicolour palette used by its hip new designers.

Whether in Brussels or Bruges, you will be able to eat well. Belgian cuisine is amongst the finest in Europe. Having lived in the shadow of France for long enough, Belgium started to market its food and drink in the 1980s and the reception has fostered greater confidence. Whether it is a roll and hot chocolate to start the day, a waffle and coffee mid-morning, a main meal at midday or *frites* bought from a stall in the middle of the night, food is taken seriously by the Belgians. To make a generalisation, traditional cooking in Bruges is peasant food, with big portions of stews like *waterzooi*, or of fresh seafood, mussels being the signature dish. Cooking in Brussels, by contrast, is often more cosmopolitan and more refined.

For all their similarities, the differences between Brussels and Bruges are what grabs the headlines. Although both are conservative and predominantly Catholic cities, and less than an hour's drive or train ride apart, the rivalry

Regional variations

It's not just language that divides Belgians into their regions – there are regional parliaments as well as the national parliament. Great efforts are made to avoid showing favouritism, often with absurd results: when money was allocated for roads in Flanders, for instance, Walloons received identical funding, even though this resulted in one motorway ending in the middle of a field.

between the Flemish and the French-speaking Walloons continues. The first time Sylvie took me to Belgium, we arrived in Brussels by train.

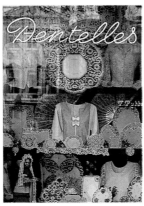

At the station newsagent, Sylvie offered a greeting in Flemish, only to be told that she would not be served speaking in *that* language. It is one of many examples of the tension between the French- and Flemish-speaking communities (the German-speakers in the east are a minority). Flemish (basically Dutch with local dialects) is the official language of Bruges, while Brussels is a bilingual city. As a precaution against causing offence, you are strongly urged to speak English or French to the French-speaking Belgians.

Fabrics and lace

In the 13th century, Belgium was already famous for woven fabrics and intricate tapestries, made from English wool and exported as far as the Orient. By the 16th century, Brussels in particular was renowned for the fine quality of its lace. Lace remains one of the most popular traditional souvenirs of Brussels and Bruges (► 70).

Sylvie first took me 'home' to Bruges in mid-winter. We went for a walk one Sunday afternoon and as we passed closed shops and cafés, empty streets, leafless trees and still canals, I understood why the writer George Rodenbach had called the city 'Bruges la morte' (dead Bruges). When I returned in mid-summer Bruges was transformed, there was not a moment's solitude to be had and people were talking about how Bruges had become a victim of its own popularity.

The reason for Bruges' popularity is obvious as soon as you reach the centre. Because it went into such a spectacular decline in the early 16th century, the city was never redeveloped and so is one of Europe's best-preserved medieval cities. Now, its wealth of medieval art and architecture generates considerable income.

Bruges is an easy place to visit. Distances are small, the city is ringed with parks and cut through by canals. Set this against a backdrop of medieval buildings, add horse-drawn carriages, tuneful bells, and treats like chocolates and mussels, and you have the perfect place to step back in time for a few days.

THE CITIES IN FIGURES

BRUSSELS

POPULATION
- 1991: 954,045 Belgians in Brussels
- 80 per cent of Bruxellois are French-speakers, 20 per cent Flemish
- One in four people living in Brussels is a foreigner
- 1995: Visitors (tourists and businessmen) spent 5,040,390 nights in Brussels

FOOD AND DRINK
- Brussels has around 1800 restaurants
- 1000 beers offered at Chez Moeder Lambic Bar (not all in stock at the same time)

ENVIRONMENT
- 13.8 per cent of Brussels is green, making it the world's second greenest capital (after Washington)

FIRST
- First train railway track on mainland Europe (1835, inaugurated by King Leopold I)

BRUGES

POPULATION
- Around 120,000 people live in Bruges and surrounding parishes

TOURISM
- Bruges is Belgium's No 1 tourist destination
- It attracts some 2.5 million visitors each year
- 1995: Visitors (tourists and businessmen) spent about a million nights in Bruges

HERITAGE
- More than 150 monuments in the city have been protected

CHRONOLOGIES

BRUSSELS

AD 695   Brocsella (Brussels) is first mentioned on the trade route between Cologne and Flanders

979   Charles, Duke of Lorraine, moves into his new fortress on the island of Saint-Géry (central Brussels). The date is now taken as the official founding of the city

1459   Philip the Good, having inherited Flanders and Burgundy, brings Brabant and Holland under his control and settles in Brussels

1515   Charles V, soon to become Holy Roman Emperor and King of Spain and the Netherlands, arrives in Brussels. As emperor, he resides in the city from 1520 to 1522 and 1530 to 1540

1568   The beheading of the Counts of Egmont and Horne in the Grand'Place sparks a revolt which leads to the independence of the United Province of the Netherlands, but not of present-day Belgium

1695   French forces bombard Brussels, destroying some 4000 buildings. In the Grand'Place, only the Town Hall tower survives intact

1789–90   The Brabançon Revolution leads to a confederation of the United Belgian States and a constitution along the lines of the new American Constitution, until Brussels falls to the French

1815   After Napoleon Bonaparte's defeat at the Battle of Waterloo, Brussels reverts to the Dutch

1830   The Belgian Revolution begins at Brussels' Théâtre de la Monnaie. It leads to independence and the crowning of Leopold of Saxe-Coburg as King of the Belgians

1957   Brussels becomes headquarters of the EEC

1967   Brussels becomes headquarters of NATO

BRUGES

3rd century AD	A settlement called Bryggja is established, its name referring to its feature: a bridge over the water, around which a town later grows to protect the crossing
1127	The first walls go up around Bruges
1297	Bruges' second ramparts are built
1302	A French army is sent to take control of Flanders, but is defeated by an army of Flemish craftsmen and peasants at the Battle of the Golden Spurs. By this time, Bruges has become one of the world's great trading cities
1303	The first-known procession of the Holy Blood, brought from Jerusalem in 1150. The procession through the streets has been repeated on Ascension Day (► 60) ever since
1348–9	The Black Death kills about a quarter of the population of Flanders
1384	Philip the Bold, Duke of Burgundy, inherits Flanders and ushers in a period of great cultural and political change
1468	Charles the Bold, Duke of Burgundy and son of Philip the Good, marries Margaret of York in Damme. The celebrations, held at Bruges, last more than a week and are still remembered to this day in the colourful five-yearly Pageant of the Golden Tree (► 60)
1488	An uprising against Archduke Maximillian leads to his kidnap and detention in Bruges. The reprisals begin the steady decline of the city
1516	Genoese and Florentine traders, who had set up business ventures in Bruges under a treaty of 1395, move to Antwerp
1898	Flemish is officially recognised as the country's joint-language with French

11

People & Events from History

Heroes Jan Breydel and Pieter de Coninck

Famous modern Belgians

King Albert (crowned in 1993)

King Baudouin I (reigned 1951–93)

Jacques Brel, master of the *chanson*

Hugo Claus, Nobel literature prize nominee, author of *The Sorrow of Belgium*

Jean-Claude van Damme, action-movie star

Johnny Halliday, rock star

Anne Teresa de Keersmaeker, dance protégée of Maurice Béjart

Eddy Merckx, bicycle hero

Toots Thielemans, Mr Jazz

JAN BREYDEL & PIETER DE CONINCK

In the centre of Bruges' Market Square stands a statue of two men. On 18 May 1302, Jan Breydel, a butcher, and Pieter de Coninck, a one-eyed weaver led an uprising against occupying French forces. An army was sent from France in reprisal, but was defeated on 11 July that year at the Battle of the Golden Spurs, in which Pieter also took part. The two men entered local folklore as Flemish heroes, with Jan embodying power and Pieter conscience. Their story was romanticised in 19th-century popular novels and their statue (1887) became a rallying-point for Flemish nationalists. The statue continues to be looked after by the city's Breydel and De Coninck Committee.

JAN VAN EYCK

One of the masters of Renaissance painting and generally credited as the father of Flemish painters, Van Eyck (c1390–1441) mastered the technique of perspective well ahead of his Italian contemporaries. As well being a painter, Van Eyck was also a diplomat and chancellor to King Philip the Good. Like film director Alfred Hitchcock, he is known to have included little self-portraits into his pictures. In one of his most famous works, the *Arnolfini Wedding Portrait*, the artist can be seen in the mirror.

LEOPOLD II

The second King of the Belgians, Leopold II (1865–1909) reshaped Brussels, laying broad new avenues from the historic centre to the royal domain and palace. The Cinquantenaire complex and its Arc de Triomphe, which celebrated fifty years of Belgian independence, shows his ambition. But he will also be remembered as the ruler of the Belgian Congo, a territory almost half the size of Europe, which was 'offered' by the explorer Henry Morton Stanley. Leopold ruled the Congo as his personal domain, in a reign that was marked by mass murder and atrocities. In 1908, a year before his death, Leopold was forced to hand over administration of his Congo to the Belgian parliament.

BRUSSELS & BRUGES

how to organise your time

ITINERARIES

Most museums and sights in Belgium close over lunch time. Many museums close on Mondays in Brussels and on Tuesdays in Bruges. As opening times of smaller museums can be erratic, make sure you check them before visiting. Both cities can easily be explored on foot.

ITINERARY ONE **BRUSSELS**

Morning Start by exploring the different guildhouses on the Grand'Place (► 28) and check the times for the morning guided tour of the Hôtel de Ville (► 29). If there is a wait, join the crowds staring at Manneken Pis (► 27) or visit the Museum of the City of Brussels (► 50).

Lunch A light lunch in the art-nouveau café Le Falstaff (► 68) or in one of the restaurants overlooking the Grand'Place.

Afternoon Walk through the rue des Bouchers and the elegant Galeries St Hubert up to the cathedral of St Michael and Ste Gudule (► 36). On the way back, visit the Centre Belge de la Bande Dessinée in the Horta-designed Magazins Waucquez (► 37). In the early evening, take a stroll past Brussels' famous cafés (► 68).

ITINERARY TWO **BRUSSELS**

Morning Start with the neighbouring museums of Classical and Modern Art (► 32–33) and a stroll through the place Royale (► 34) to the place du Grand Sablon, with its impressive Church of Notre Dame du Sablon and the pretty gardens of the Petit Sablon (► 30).

Wittamer patisserie in the Grand Sablon

14

Lunch	There are plenty of possibilities for lunch in this area.
Afternoon	Take a tram to the Musée de Victor Horta (► 31, check opening times). Discover some of the city's finest art-nouveau architecture in the Saint-Gilles area and then walk back to the shopping haven of the avenue Louise (► 35).

ITINERARY THREE   **BRUGES**

Morning	Climb the belfry on the Markt (► 46) for a good overview of Bruges and the lie of the land. Continue to the Burg (► 47) and visit the Brugse Vrije museum and the astonishing Gothic room in the Town Hall, and then go on to the Heilig Bloedbasiliek(► 48).
Lunch	Walk to the Huidenvettersplein where there are several restaurants.
Afternoon	Follow the Dijver to the Groeninge Museum (► 45) and after that the Gruuthuse Museum (► 44). Wander around the garden towards the Onze-Lieve-Vrouwekerk (► 43). In the evening, walk along the romantic floodlit canals or take a boat trip.

ITINERARY FOUR   **BRUGES**

Morning	Start the day at Kathedraal St Salvator (► 40) and follow with some of the best of Flemish art in the Memling Museum (► 42). Walk to the Begijnhof (► 41) and enjoy the quiet.
Lunch	Have lunch in the Wijngaardplein or take a picnic to the park overlooking the Minnewater (► 57).
Afternoon	Walk along the canals (► 59). The Dijver, Groenerei and Verversdijk lead to the Potterierei where you can visit the lesser-known Museum Onze-Lieve-Vrouw Ter Potterie (► 51). Return along the Kruisvest, and visit the Sint-Janshuysmolen windmill and its museum (► 55).

WALKS

THE CRADLE OF BRUSSELS, FROM MANNEKEN TO JANNEKEN PIS

THE SIGHTS

- Grand'Place (► 28)
- Plaques to Charles Buls (Mayor and restorer of the Grand'Place) and Everard't Servaes (14th century defender of city's liberties)
- Manneken Pis (► 27)
- Eglise Notre-Dame du Bon-Secours
- Janneken Pis (panel ► 27)

INFORMATION

Distance c1.5km
Time 1–2 hours
Start point Grand'Place

➕ E7

🚇 Gare Centrale/Centraal Station

🚋 Tram 23, 52, 55, 56, 81 (Bourse/Beurs)

End point Rue des Bouchers

➕ E7

Fish restaurants abound near place St Catherine

Leave the Grand'Place via rue Charles Buls, passing two plaques under the arcade. Walk along rue de l'Etuve leading to Manneken Pis, then turn right along rue des Grands-Carmes to the Marché du Charbon. Walk past Eglise Notre-Dame du Bon-Secours to the boulevard Anspach. There turn right, walk to the traffic lights and cross left into rue des Riches Claires with a 17th-century church. Turn right into the street leading to place Saint-Géry where, immediately left, a passageway leads to the back of the church and the original site of the River Senne.

Return to the square where a renovated 19th-century covered market has a plaque indicating the site of Brussels' beginnings. Walk along rue du Pont de la Carpe and then left into rue Antoine Dansaert with restaurants and clothes shops. Take a right into rue du Vieux Marché aux Grains, leading to place St Catherine, built on a basin of the old port of Brussels, which explains the presence of a fish market. Walk past the Tour Noire, part of the first city wall, back to boulevard Anspach and cross over into rue de l'Evêque to place de la Monnaie with the Théâtre de la Monnaie. Take a right into rue des Fripiers and left into rue Grétry which becomes rue des Bouchers, where Janneken Pis is signed.

LESSER-KNOWN BRUGES

Leave the Markt along Philipstockstraat, turn left into Cordoeaniersstraat to St Janplein. On the other side take St Jansstraat to St Maartensplein, with the baroque church of Sint-Walburgakerk (► 53). Walk along the left side of the church in Hoornstraat to the Verversdijk, then turn right and cross over the bridge to come into St Annakerkstraat, with the Church of St Anna, dating to the 17th century. At the back of the church, cross Jeruzalemstraat towards the Jeruzalemkerk (► 53) on the corner. Next door is the Kantcentrum (✉ Peperstraat 3), where you can see how lace is made.

Lace making

From the Jeruzalemkerk turn into Balstraat and then Rolweg, with the Museum voor Volkskunde (► 51). Cross Rolweg to Carmersstraat and turn right. No 85 is the dome of the Engels Klooster, No 174 is the old Schuttersgilde Sint-Sebastiaan, and straight ahead on Kruisvest is the Sint-Janshuysmolen windmill (► 55). Take a right along Kruisvest. On the corner with Rolweg is a museum dedicated to the Flemish poet Guido Gezelle (1830–99), and further along, the Bonne Chiere windmill (► 39). At Kruispoort (► 39), turn right into Langestraat. At No 47 is the Brewery Museum (entrance ✉ Verbrand Nieuwland, 10 ☎ 33 06 99 ◉ Jun–Sep Wed–Sun 2–5). Before the end of Langestraat, turn left over a bridge into Predikherenstraat, cross another bridge and turn right to Groenerei (► 59), one of Bruges' loveliest corners. At the end of the street is Vismarkt, with a fish market (Tuesday to Saturday mornings). To the right an alley under the arch leads to the Burg (► 47).

THE SIGHTS

- Markt
- Sint-Walburgakerk
- Sint-Annakerk
- Jeruzalemkerk
- Museum voor Volkskunde
- Engels Klooster
- Windmills
- Kruispoort
- Brewery Museum
- Groenerei
- Vismarkt
- Burg

INFORMATION

Distance 3km
Time 2–3 hours
Start point Markt
⊞ bIII
🚌 Bus 1, 2, 3, 4, 8, 11, 13, 17
End point Burg
⊞ bIII
🚌 Bus 1, 2, 3, 4, 8, 11, 13, 17

EVENING STROLLS

A BAR CRAWL IN BRUSSELS

Start with a typical Brussels' apéritif of *half en half*, half champagne and half white wine, on the terrace of the Metropole Hotel (➤ 85) on the place de Brouckère. Leave the hotel to the right and after 20m turn right into the Passage du Nord. At the end of the passage, turn right again into rue Neuve/Nieuwstraat towards the place de la Monnaie/Muntplein where you can try the house beer in La Lunette (➤ 68). Turn right off the *place* onto the rue du Fossé aux Loups or Wolvengracht

Choosing a restaurant

with Café Old Paris, a real 'brown' café (No 29), turn right again past the SAS Radisson Hotel with the famous bar, A la Mort Subite (➤ 68) opposite. Walk through Galeries St Hubert, taking the first passage to the right into rue des Bouchers, then first left past the old-fashioned *estaminet* of the Théâtre de Toone (➤ 81). Walk towards the Marché aux Herbes/Grasmarkt and on to the Grand'Place, where you take a right into rue au Beurre. To the left of the Bourse is the Falstaff terrace and to the right is the Cirio.

BRUGES BY NIGHT

From the Markt walk along Steenstraat to Simon Stevinplein, turn left into Mariastraat, and at the end of the street admire the tower of the Onze-Lieve-Vrouwekerk (➤ 43) and look into the courtyard of the Gruuthuse Museum (➤ 44). Walk along the Dijver and cross over onto Rozenhoedkaai, where you take the first passage left leading to Huidenvettersplein. Walk past the Vismarkt along the romantic Steenhouwersdijk (Groenerei). Cross over the bridge to the left into Meestraat and then left in Hoogstraat. At the end admire the Burg (➤ 47).

ORGANISED SIGHTSEEING

BRUSSELS

ARAU (Atelier de recherche et d'Action Urbaines) ✉ 55, boulevard Adolphe Max/Adolphe Maxlaan ☎ 219 3345 *Brussels 1900*, a coach tour, shows art-nouveau architecture and visits some Horta buildings not always open to the general public (🕐 Mar–Nov, Sat). *Alternative Brussels* (🕐 1st Sat of month Mar–Nov) is a coach tour through downtown and the industrial districts explaining the city's history. Every second Saturday of the month there is a tour of Brussels' most beautiful parks and squares and every third Saturday a coach tour visits art-deco buildings. Tours are in French, although English guides can be arranged.

Brussels City Tours ✉ De Boeck 8, rue de la Colline/Heuvelstraat (Grand'Place) ☎ 513 7744 Daily tours of the city, starting with a guided walk on the Grand'Place, followed by a bus ride around Brussels' main sights (3 hours).

Discovering Brussels

From July to September Bruxelles Découvertes (rue Hôtel des Monnaies/Munthofstraat 157 ☎ 539 0434) organises the Chemins d'été, 200 tours on foot, by cycle, car, bus or boat, discovering hidden treasures in and around Brussels. Detailed brochures from the Tourist Office on the Grand'Place. At the same address, Itinéraires also offers walks in the footsteps of famous residents like Bruegel, Hugo, Tintin and Jacques Brel.

BRUGES

Bruges by Boat A charming way to explore the city is to take a boat trip on the canals (▶ 59). Trips start from the Dijver, Katelijnestraat, Wollestraat, Huidenvettersplein and Vismarkt (32 min). (🕐 Daily Mar–Oct, weekends Dec, closed Jan.)

Bruges with Bart Info/tickets ✉ Bookshop de Reyghere, Markt 12 ☎ 34 37 09 Guided bicycle tours of the main and lesser-known sights, from March to October at 1.45. Bart also organises a daily four-hour cycle tour of the country around Bruges,

Horse-drawn cabs Every day, from March to November, 10–6, horse-drawn cabs tour the city centre, starting from the Burg (35 min).

City Tour Brugge A coach leaves the Markt hourly for a 50-minute tour of Bruges' sights (in English, French, German, Dutch, Spanish, Italian or Japanese).

busstop: markt - every hour

Excursions

FROM BRUSSELS TO WATERLOO AND LEUVEN

WATERLOO

Just 20km south of Brussels is the famous battlefield where on 18 June 1815 the Duke of Wellington defeated Napoleon Bonaparte. The Butte de Lion, a grass-covered pyramid erected by the Dutch a decade later to mark the spot where William of Orange was wounded, is what most people come for and few are disappointed. At the foot of the mound is the Visitor Centre with a Waterloo panorama. It is well worth climbing the 226 steps for the views from the top. The Wellington Museum (☎ 02-354 5954) in the inn where the Duke was lodged, shows memorabilia from the battle, including an officer's wooden leg. The Museum of Caillou (☎ 02-384 2424), in a farm where Napoleon spent the night, also has a few battlefield souvenirs.

LEUVEN

Leuven is a pleasant Flemish university town. The 15th-century Town Hall on the Grote Markt is typical of the late Brabant Gothic style, while the Tafelrond is a neo-Gothic reconstruction of 15th-century houses. St Peter's Church has two wonderful triptychs by the 15th-century painter Dirk Bouts. The grandest of all the cafés around the Grote Markt is Café Gambrinus which has pre-art-nouveau frescos. Near by is St Michielskerk, a marvel of 17th-century baroque, while the Great Beguinage is a village in itself with 17th and 18th-century houses, now part of Belgium's largest university, the Catholic University of Leuven. The city tends to be quiet in June when students are taking their exams but comes back to life in summer.

Waterloo: the battlefield. Inset: statue topping the Butte de Lion

FROM BRUGES TO DAMME AND KNOKKE

DAMME

When the old port in Bruges dried out after the estuary silted up, the focus of trade shifted to Damme, a small and pleasant town. Only 7km from Bruges it is a popular excursion by foot, bike or boat, with culinary delights at the end: restaurants and tea rooms offer local specialities such as *anguilles au vert* (river eel in herb sauce), Damme sausages, Damme Tart, and a semi-hard Damme cheese. On the main square stands the 19th-century statue of Jacob van Maerlant (1235–1300), the Flemish poet, who wrote his best work in Damme. The Gothic Town Hall (1464) has two punishment stones on the corner and some fine mouldings inside the Council Hall and the Vierschaere. The Church of Our Lady dates back to the 14th century, but the aisles, nave and transept were pulled down in 1725. From the top of its 45m-high tower there are magnificent views over town and country. The towpath by the canal from Bruges to Damme is perfect for an afternoon walk.

KNOKKE

Close to the Dutch border, Knokke is Belgium's most elegant seaside resort, with many turn-of-the-century villas and small hotels along its quiet green lanes. Het Zoute, its chic neighbourhood, is where the Brussels and Antwerp bourgeoisie likes to be seen in the summer and at weekends. It is also a shopper's paradise with some of Belgium's most elegant boutiques, jewellers and many art galleries. The beaches are clean and get wider the further you go towards the border with Holland. The Zwin nature reserve is a bird-watcher's heaven.

Damme windmill

INFORMATION

Damme
Distance 7km
Journey time Bus 15 min, boat 35 min

🚌 Bus 799 from Bruges station

⛴ by boat the 'Lamme Goedzak' Apr–Sep
✉ Noorweegse Kaai 31
☎ reservations: 050-35 33 19 🕐 from Bruges 10, 12, 2, 4:20 and 6; from Damme 9:15, 11, 1, 3, 5:20

ℹ Tourist Office ✉ Town Hall, Damme ☎ 050-35 33 19

Knokke
Distance 20km
Journey time 25 min by train

🚆 Frequent trains from Bruges to Knokke

🚌 Bus 788/1 from Bruges station or t'Zand

ℹ Tourist Office ✉ Zeedijk-Knokke 660
☎ 050-63 03 80

WHAT'S ON

In Brussels, the daily newspapers have listings of what's on in the city. *The Bulletin* is the only English-language weekly. It has a 'What's On' supplement with good listings, but most of it is devoted to business and EU matters. *Humo* has listings in Flemish while *Kiosk* covers nightlife, concerts and exhibitions in French. Tickets are usually available at the appropriate venues. Tickets for many events can also be purchased from the Tourist Office Brussels ☒ Grand'Place ☎ 513 8940 or FNAC ☒ City2 rue Neuve ☎ 209 2211.

The monthly *Exit* magazine, available (free) at the Bruges Tourist Office, has a detailed calendar of events.

JANUARY	*Brussels International Film Festival*
APRIL–MAY	*Brussels–Europe weeks.*
	Brussels Royal greenhouses open to the public (► 54)
MAY	Ascension Day, Bruges, Procession of the Holy Blood (► 60).
	End of May, *Brussels Jazz Marathon*: jazz concerts on the Grand'Place and 60 city bars.
	Last Sunday in May, Brussels, 20-km run past the major sights.
	May/June–September, Brussels, *Summer Festival* with good classical concerts
JUNE	Mid-June, every five years, re-enactment of the Battle of Waterloo at Waterloo (☎ 354 9910)
JULY	First week, *Brussels Ommegang* (► 60).
	2nd weekend in July, Bruges, *Cactus Festival* with open-air concerts in the Minnewater Park.
	Mid-July–mid-August, Brussels, *Foire du Midi*, largest fair in Europe with over 2km of attractions and food stalls.
	21 July, Brussels, *National Day* festivities
AUGUST	9 August, Brussels, raising of the Meeiboom (Maypole) (► 60).
	Mid-August, Brussels, *Floral carpet* on the Grand'Place in even-numbered years.
	Every three years in Bruges, *Reiefeesten* or Festival of the Canals: walk along the canals to see historical scenes enacted against the background of the monuments
SEPTEMBER	Every five years in Bruges, the *Gouden Boomstoet* Pageant of the Golden Tree (► 60).
	2nd, 3rd weekend, *Heritage Days*, hundreds of houses and monuments open their doors to the general public
OCTOBER–DECEMBER	Brussels, *Europalia* cultural events

BRUSSELS & BRUGES's
top 25 sights

The sights are shown on the maps on the inside front cover and on the inside back cover, numbered **1–25** *from west to east across the cities*

LA BASILIQUE DE KOEKELBERG

DID YOU KNOW?

- Koekelberg is dedicated to the nation's martyrs
- 44,000 Belgians died in World War I
- 700,000 more were deported to Germany
- Most Belgians are Catholic but in the 16th century many became Lutherans and Calvinists
- The first Lutherans were burned in Brussels in 1523
- Under the Edict of Blood up to 30,000 people were executed

INFORMATION

- ✠ C5
- ✉ 1 parvis de la Basilique, 1083 Brussels
- ☎ 425 8822
- 🕐 Easter–31 Oct, Mon–Sat 8–6; 1 Nov–Easter, Mon–Sat 8–5
- 🍴 None
- 🚇 Simonis
- 🚌 87
- ♿ Few
- 🎫 Free (guided tours – moderate)
- ❓ Guided tours of dome Mon–Fri 11 and 3, Sat & Sun 2 and 5:45

"Approaching Brussels from the north or west, the city is dominated by a dramatic domed building. The National Basilica of Koekelberg was intended as a symbol of unification, but the result is strangely unmoving and cold."

The building Koekelberg, more properly known as the Basilique Nationale de Sacré Coeur, is the world's largest art deco-style church, a fitting monument to the Sacred Heart and to the nation's martyrs to whom it is dedicated. Construction began in 1935 but the church was not finished until 1979. The result is an enormous building, 167m by 89m, with a soaring dome 22m in diameter. On a dull day it can seem a cold and gloomy place, but the scale of the choir is impressive and there are several pretty chapels. Stained-glass windows from the 1930s and 1940s are labelled. The statue of Our Lady is worth seeking out. Amongst Koekelberg's other attractions are the centre for Christian cartoons, with a shop selling magazines and T-shirts, and a pilgrimage office.

Its significance Rather than being a factor in the city's and country's unification, Koekelberg seems to show up the divisions between the Flemish and Walloons, as when the Pope visited Brussels. The story has it that although known for kissing the ground on arrival in a country, the Pope was unable to do so at Brussels airport for fear of being seen to show favour to the Flemish, in whose territory the airport lies. So it was not until he reached Koekelberg that he dared to bend down and kiss the ground. Separate Flemish and French services are held here, so in spite of the intention to make Koekelberg a symbol of unification, even here the communities are divided.

HEYSEL

❝*To commemorate Belgium's 100th birthday in 1930, Heysel/Heizel was chosen as the site for the Centenary Stadium and the Palais du Centenaire. To many, the name recalls a sombre episode in football history, but there is some fun to be had as well.*❞

The Atomium The Atomium (1) was designed in steel and aluminium for Expo '58 by Andre Waterkeyn. Its nine balls represent the atoms of a metal crystal enlarged 165 billion times. Inside the huge balls is the Biogenium exhibition covering the history of medicine, laboratories, virology, cells and genetics. The exhibition may be rather dull but the panoramic view from the top of the atoms is spectacular.

Stranger landmarks After the Universal Exhibition in Paris in 1900, King Leopold II wanted to have his own chinoiseries, for which he commissioned Parisian architect Alexandre Marcel. For the Japanese Tower (2), the Entrance Pavilion to the Japanese Pagoda from the Paris Exhibition was brought to Brussels. The splendid Chinese Pavilion (3), with a façade that was carved in Shanghai, houses a fine collection of porcelain from the late 17th to the early 19th centuries. Both pavilions are hidden in beautiful woodlands.

Trade space The Palais de Centenaire, built, like the Stadium, by Van Neck, is a series of art-deco-style halls which forms the core of the Trade Mart. Ten more palaces have been built, making Brussels a unique European venue for international trade fairs.

HIGHLIGHTS

- The Atomium
- Japanese Tower
- Chinese Pavilion

INFORMATION

➕ (1) D2, (2 & 3) F2

✉ (1) boulevard du Centenaire/Eeuwfeestlaan; (2 & 3) 44 avenue van Praet

☎ (1) 477 0977 (2) 268 1608

🕐 (1) Apr–Aug: daily 9–8, Sep–Mar: daily 10–6; (2 & 3) Tue–Sun 10–4:40. Closed Mon; 1 Jan, 1 & 11 Nov, 25 Dec

🍴 (1) Restaurant Mon–Sat (££)

🚊 Heysel/Heizel

🚌 (1) Tram 23, 81; bus 84, 89; (2 & 3) tram 19, 23, 32, 92, bus 53

♿ (1, 2, 3) None

💰 (1) Expensive, (2 & 3) moderate

🔗 Bruparck (► 56), parc de Laeken (► 57)

Top: the Atomium.
Left: the Japanese Tower

3

LES MAROLLES

Top: junk market in the place du Jeu de Balle.

❝*Dwarfed by the Palais de Justice and hemmed in by the luxurious quarter of the Sablon, the Marolles are a reminder of popular Brussels. The smoky cafés often do not bother to close at all as the junk market attracts the early birds.*❞

The heart and soul of Brussels The Marolles developed in the 17th century as a residential area for craftsmen working on the palaces and grand houses of the Upper City. It remained a lively working-class area until the 1870s, when the River Senne was covered and many artisans moved further out. In the 19th century, part of the Marolles was demolished to make way for the imposing Palais de Justice. In the shadow of this symbol of law and order, the district declined and became a crumbling haven for the city's poor and Maghrebi immigrants from north-west Africa.

Where to go The Marolles stretches roughly from the Porte de Hal to the Eglise Notre-Dame-de-la-Chapelle/Kapellekerk, with the rue Blaes and the rue Haute/Hoogstraat as its main thoroughfares. The streets around the place du Jeu de Balle/Vossenplein are full of snack-bars, 'brown cafés' and junk shops. The junk market, held on the place du Jeu de Balle, is the place to sniff out the atmosphere, especially on Sunday mornings, the liveliest time for trading.

Property speculation The Marolles is changing quickly as property speculators, art galleries, and the fashionable crowd move in. Neither the decreasing number of indigenous inhabitants nor the new immigrant families have the money to save their homes from falling down but action groups are now working for the preservation of the Marolles and the restoration of its buildings.

MANNEKEN PIS

❝It might be easy to miss this little fellow, a strange mascot for a city, if it were not for the busloads of tourists who gather in front of it to have their picture taken.❞

The cheeky cherub Manneken Pis, meaning literally 'the pissing little boy', is one of Brussels' more amusing symbols. The tiny bronze statuette, less than 60cm high, was created by Jérôme Duquesnoy the Elder in 1619. Known then as 'Petit Julien', it has since become a legend. One story claims that the Julien on whom the statue was modelled was the son of Duke Gottfried of Lorraine, another that the statue urinated on a bomb fuse to save the Town Hall from destruction. But in fact very little is known about its origins.

Body wounds The statue has often been vandalised. He was kidnapped by the English in 1745 and two years later the French took him away. In 1817 a French convict ran off with the statue, but it was later found in pieces. Those fragments were used to make the mould for the present statue. Even now he remains a temptation: he has been removed several times by drunk or angry students.

An extravagant wardrobe The French king Louis XV gave him a richly embroidered robe and the cross of Louis XIV, as reparation for the bad behaviour of his soldiers in 1747. Manneken Pis now has hundreds of costumes, on show in the Museum of the City of Brussels (➤ 50–51).

DID YOU KNOW?

- In 1985 feminists demanded a female version of Manneken Pis and commissioned Janneken Pis (✉ Impasse de la Fidelité off the Rue des Bouchers/ Beenhouwersstraat)
- Every 13th of September Manneken Pis wears the uniform of a sergeant in the Regiment of Welsh Guards to celebrate the liberation of Brussels in 1944

INFORMATION

- ✚ E7
- ✉ Corner of rue de l'Etuve/Stoofstraat and rue du Chêne/Eikstraat
- 🚉 Gare Centrale/Centraal Station
- 🚊 Tram 23, 52, 55, 56, 81 (Bourse/Beurs)
- ♿ Free
- ↔ Grand'Place/Grote Markt (➤ 28), Hôtel de Ville/Stadhuis (➤ 29), Costume and Lace Museum (➤ 50), Museum of the City of Brussels (➤ 50–51)
- ❓ See sign at the statue for the dates when it is dressed up

Top and left: two of Manneken Pis's luxurious costumes

5

GRAND' PLACE

HIGHLIGHTS

- Hôtel de Ville
- La Maison du Roi, now the Museum of the City of Brussels
- Elegant dome of Roi d'Espagne
- Bronze plaques of Charles Buls and Everard 't Serclaes in arcade to left of Hôtel de Ville, stroked for good luck
- Floral carpet, Aug every other year (1998 etc)

INFORMATION

- ✚ E7
- 🍴 Several restaurants (£–£££)
- 🚇 Gare Centrale/ Centraal Station
- 🚊 Tram 23, 52, 55, 56, 81 (Bourse/Beurs)
- ♿ Good
- 🎟 Free
- ↔ Manneken Pis (► 27), Centre Belge de la Bande Dessinée (► 37), Museum of the City of Brussels (► 50–51), Costume and Lace Museum (► 50)
- ❓ Daily flower market; bird market on Sun; mid-Dec Christmas Fair with Christmas tree, crib, live animals, shopping, food, concerts

"What a joy to walk out in the morning and watch the early sun light up the gilded Gothic, Renaissance and baroque façades which pack together round this delightful square."

The centre of Brussels The Grand'Place/Grote Markt is still the one sight in Brussels that all tourists come to admire. By the 11th century the market place was already the focal point of commerce and in the 13th century the three first halls – for bread, cloth and meat – were built on the site of the Maison du Roi. Commercial activity soon spread to the streets around the square, still evoked today in the street names (Butchers' Street, Herb Market, Cheese Market Street). Brussels prospered and by the 15th century the Hôtel de Ville (► 29) was the proud symbol of its new importance. The square was almost totally destroyed by a French bombardment in 1695, but was entirely rebuilt by the guilds in less than five years.

The guildhouses Nos 1–2 Au Roi d'Espagne – bakers' guild; No 3 La Brouette (Wheelbarrow) – tallow-makers' guild; No 4 Le Sac – joiners', coopers' and cabinet-makers' guild; No 5 La Louve (She-wolf) – house of the Archer; No 6 Le Cornet – boatmen's guild; No 7 Le Renard (Fox) – haberdashers' guild; No 9 Le Cygne (Swan) – butchers' guild, where in 1847 Marx and Engels wrote *The Communist Manifesto*; No 10 L'Arbre d'Or (golden tree) – brewers' guild; Nos 13–19 – Houses of the Dukes of Brabant; Nos 24–25 La Chaloupe d'Or (golden galleon) – tailors' guild; Nos 26–27 Le Pigeon – painters' guild, where Victor Hugo stayed in 1852; and Nos 29–33 Maison du Roi, called Broodhuis in Flemish – never belonged to a king but to the bakers' guild.

HÔTEL DE VILLE

❝Had the architect of the elegant bell-tower of the Hôtel de Ville known how much we admire his creation today, perhaps he would not have thrown himself off it. He committed suicide because the lower part of his tower seemed slightly off the centre of the façade.❞

Top: town hall façade.
Above: St Michael

A Gothic masterpiece Flanders and Brabant have a wealth of Gothic town halls, but the Brussels Hôtel de Ville is probably the most beautiful of all. It was started in the spring of 1402 and in 1444 the right wing was added. The octagonal 96m-high tower, added later by architect Jan Van Ruysbroeck, bears a gilt statue of the Archangel St Michael. The top of the tower, 400 steps up, gives the best views over the Grand'Place and the heart of Brussels. Most of the sculptures adorning the façade of the Town Hall, are 19th-century replacements of 14th- and 15th-century originals, now in the Museum of the City of Brussels (➤ 50). The courtyard has two 18th-century fountains representing Belgium's most important rivers, the Meuse (to the left), and Scheldt (on the right).

The Grand Staircase The recently renovated Grand Staircase carries the busts of all the mayors of Brussels since Belgian independence in 1830. Count Jacques Lalaing made the impressive paintings on the walls in 1893.

The Gothic Hall This was formerly the Council Chamber, once used for official ceremonies. The 19th-century tapestries on the walls are interesting for their depiction of the city's main guilds and their crafts. The windows are decorated with the coats of arms of Brussels' guilds and noble families. The tour includes some of the offices of the mayors and magistrates.

HIGHLIGHTS

- Grand Staircase
- belltower
- magnificent tapestries

INFORMATION

- ✚ E7
- ☎ In tourist office: 513 8940
- 🔄 Guided tours only, in Dutch, English and German (check with tourist office for times); groups Thu only
- 🍴 Plenty near by (£–£££)
- 🚊 Tram 23, 52, 55, 56, 81 (Bourse/Beurs)
- ♿ Good
- 💰 Moderate
- ↔ Manneken Pis (➤ 27), Museum of the City of Brussels (➤ 50–51)

29

7

LE SABLON

HIGHLIGHTS

- Eglise de Notre Dame du Sablon
- Statues on the place du Petit Sablon/Kleine Zavel Plein
- Antique market and shops
- Garden behind Palais d'Egmont
- Patisserie Wittamer

"A mecca for the antique trade, this is a charming neighbourhood to wander around or for sitting and watching the world go by from a terrace. The Petit Sablon offers the perfect background for savouring the delicacies on sale in the place du Grand Sablon."

Top: the antiques market.
Above: chocolates

INFORMATION

- ➕ E/F8
- ✉ Area around place du Grand Sablon
- ☎ Church: 511 5741
- 🕐 Church: 0–6, holidays 9–6
- 🍽 Several restaurants, cafés and tea rooms (£–£££)
- 🚊 Tram 91, 92, 93, 94; bus 20, 48
- ♿ Good
- ↔ Les Marolles (➤ 26), Musées d'Art Ancien et Moderne (➤ 32, 33), place Royal/Koningsplein (➤ 34)
- ❓ Antiques market Sat 9–6; Sun 9–2 (➤ 58); *Ommegang* procession (➤ 60)

La place du Grand Sablon/Grote Zavel Many of Brussels' 17th-century aristocracy and bourgeoisie lived in this elegant square, now the centre of the antiques trade. The Sablon Shopping Garden is the longest art gallery in Belgium and Patisserie Wittamer (➤ 74) sells wonderful gâteaux, biscuits and chocolates.

La place du Petit Sablon/Kleine Zavel The square was commissioned in 1890 by the mayor Charles Buls. The statue of the Counts of Egmont and Horne, beheaded by the Duke of Alba because of their religion, was moved here from the Grand'Place and is surrounded by statues of famous scholars and humanists of the 16th century. Behind the garden, the 16th-century Palais d'Egmont, rebuilt in the early 20th century after a fire, is used for receptions by the Ministry of Foreign Affairs.

Eglise de Notre Dame du Sablon/Onze-Lieve-Vrouw-Ten-Zavelkerk The 15th-century church of Notre Dame du Sablon is a fine example of flamboyant Gothic architecture, built over an earlier chapel with a miraculous statue of the Virgin Mary. The choir (1435) and the stained-glass windows are particularly beautiful. Many statues, pinacles, turrets and parts of the façade were finished or restored in 19th-century neo-Gothic style.

MUSÉE DE VICTOR HORTA

❝*Many of the grand buildings designed by Victor Horta, the famous architect of the art-nouveau period, have been destroyed, but happily his own house in the rue Americaine has survived and one cannot fail to be charmed by the light and flowing lines of his architectural vision.*❞

The art-nouveau house and workspace Victor Horta (1861–1947) built the two houses on the rue Américaine, his home and studio, between 1898 and 1901. Now a museum, they clearly illustrate the break he made from the traditional town houses with large and sombre rooms. His rooms are spacious and airy, full of mirrors, white tiles and stained-glass windows. A light shaft in the middle of the house illumines a spectacular staircase, so gracious and fluid that you just want to slide down it. Horta designed every element of the house with amazing attention to detail.

Art-nouveau architecture in Saint-Gilles/Sint Gillis The wealthy residential area of Saint-Gilles still has many art-nouveau residences, although only Horta's house is officially open to the public. Wandering around the neighbourhood between the rue Defacqz and the prison one can admire several examples of this grand but short-lived style. Hankar designed the Ciambarlani (1897) and Janssens (1898) mansions at Nos 48 and 50 rue Defacqz, and his own house at No 71. On the rue Faider, at Nos 83 and 85, are houses by Roosenboom and Van Waesberghe (1900). At No 83 rue de Livourne is the private house (1912) of the architect Van Rysselberghe, who in 1894 had built the Otlet mansion at No 48 rue de Livourne. The Hannon mansion, now a photographer's gallery, at No 1 avenue de la Jonction has an impressive fresco by Paul-Albert Baudoin in the staircase.

DID YOU KNOW?

- Art nouveau originated in Britain in the 1880s but Brussels architects Paul Hankar, Henri van de Velde and especially Victor Horta made it completely their own style
- ARAU trips visit other art-nouveau houses (➤ 19)
- A brochure 'Le Guide des décors céramiques à Bruxelles de 1880 à 1940' by Chantal Declève takes in 10 walks along the most beautiful art-nouveau façades in Brussels and is available from the Tourist Office on the Grand'Place, the Horta Museum and good bookshops

INFORMATION

➕ E10

✉ 25 rue Americaine/ Amerikaanse Straat

☎ 537 1692

🕐 Tue–Sun 2–5:30. Closed Mon, hols

🚋 Tram 81, 82, 91, 92; bus 54, 60

♿ Few

💰 Expensive, double on Sat & Sun

Top: art-nouveau staircase in the Horta Museum

9

MUSÉE D'ART ANCIEN

HIGHLIGHTS

- Landscape with the Fall of Icarus and The Census at Bethlehem, Breughel
- The Ascent to Calvary and The Martyrdom of St Lievin, Rubens
- Marat Murdered in his Bath, David
- Days of September, Wappers
- The Scandalised Masks, Ensor
- The Temptation of St Antony, School of Hieronymus Bosch

INFORMATION

- E7/8
- 3 rue de la Régence/Regentschapsstraat
- 508 3211
- Tue–Sun 10–12 & 1–5. Closed Mon, 1 Jan, 1 May, 1 & 11 Nov, 25 Dec
- Cafeteria (£)
- Gare Centrale/Centraal Station or Parc/Park
- Tram 92, 93, 94; bus 20, 34, 38, 60, 71, 95, 96
- Good
- Free
- Le Sablon/Zavel (➤ 30), Musée d'Art Moderne (➤ 33), place Royale/Koningsplein (➤ 34)
- Regular exhibitions, music and readings (information from Friends of the Museum 511 4116)

"Inside a predominantly grey and dull building lies an incredibly rich collection of works of art, created between the 15th and the end of the 19th centuries. The Breughel and Rubens collections alone are worth travelling to see."

Museum history The Museum of Classical Art and the neighbouring Museum of Modern Art were founded by Napoleon Bonaparte in 1801 as the Museum of Brussels. The museum building was constructed in 1874–80 by Leopold II's colonial architect, Alphonse Balat, and completely modernised in the 1980s. Appropriately, it is connected to the Museum of Modern Art, by an underground passage.

Artistic riches The 14th to 17th centuries were a particularly rich period in Belgian art history, peaking with Memling's marvellous canvases and the bizarre visions of Hieronymus Bosch. The collection of the works of the Breughels is world-class, second only to Vienna's Kunsthistorisches Museum. Also shown are works by Van der Weyden, Bouts, Van der Goes and, amongst later artists, Jordaens and Van Dyck.

18th–19th centuries. The museum's lower level contains 19th-century works by Artan, Meunier and Navez alongside those by Courbet and Rodin. On the ground floor, the central Forum is home to a collection of 19th-century sculptures including works by Kessels, Rousseau and Rodin, while the rooms off it contain masterpieces of the Romantic and Classical movements, including work by Delacroix.

Sculpture garden The sculpture collection is less well known, but is home to an excellent and well-arranged collection.

MUSÉE D'ART MODERNE

"This museum puts modern Belgian artists in their context and many of them shine, even amongst the great European stars. It also has a reputation for staging important temporary exhibitions."

20th-century Belgians There has been a tendency to overlook Belgian artists in favour of their European or American contemporaries, so it is tempting to see something symbolic about the architecture of the Museum of Modern Art since the collection is housed in a multi-storey subterranean building adjoining the Museum of Classical Art. But by the time you have walked through the galleries of visual art, arranged chronologically (except for sculpture), you will be seeing the light.

Fauvists and Surrealists A movement that started in Paris in 1905, largely inspired by the work of van Gogh, and which was given its name by a critic who described the gallery where they exhibited as 'a cage of wild beasts', Fauvism is best represented here by the works of Rik Wouters, Auguste Oleffe and Ferdinand Schirren. Surrealism followed with its rejection of aesthetic values, growing out of the chaos of post-World War I Europe. Belgians René Magritte and Paul Delvaux stand out as two of the stars of Surrealism. Amongst the foreign artists represented here are Max Ernst and Francis Picabia.

Other movements The history of visual art in Belgium is followed as it develops through Futurism, abstract art and the 1960s' movements up to the present time. The museum also contains a collection of important works by Picasso, de Chirico, Chagall and Dali, which helps to put the Belgians in a wider context.

HIGHLIGHTS

- *L'Empire des Lumières* and others, René Magritte
- *The Flautist* and *The Woman with the Yellow Necklace*, Rik Wouters
- *In August, 1909*, Auguste Oleffe
- *The Public Voice* and *Pygmalion*, Paul Delvaux

INFORMATION

- F7
- 1–2 Place Royale/ Koningsplein
- 508 3211
- Tue–Sun 10–1, 2–5. Closed Mon, 1 Jan, 1 May, 1 & 11 Nov, 22 Dec
- Cafeteria (£)
- Gare Centrale/Centraal Station or Parc/Park
- Tram 92, 93, 94; bus 20, 34, 38, 54, 60, 71, 95, 96
- Very good
- Free
- Le Sablon/Zavel (➤ 30), Musée d'Art Ancien (➤ 32), place Royale/ Koningsplein (➤ 34)
- Regular temporary exhibitions as well as readings and music (information from Friends of the Museum ☎ 511 4116)

Top: Irène Hamoir, *Rene Magritte 1936*

33

PLACE ROYALE

HIGHLIGHTS

- Place du Musée
- Palace of Charles de Lorraine
- Place des Palais
- Fountain in the parc de Bruxelles

INFORMATION

- ✚ F7–8
- ✉ (1) place des Palais 7; (2) place Royale; (3) place des Palais
- ☎ (1) 511 5578, (2) 511 7836, (3) 551 2020
- 🕐 (1) Tue –Sun 10–4 (2) Tue–Sun 10–6, and Mon 3–6 (3) 31 Jul–30 Sep: 9:30–3:30
- 🍴 None
- 🅿 Parc/Park
- 🚋 Tram 92, 93, 94; bus 20, 34, 38, 54, 60, 71, 95, 96
- ♿ (1 & 2) None (3) good
- 🎫 (1,2 & 3) Free
- ↔ Le Sablon/Zavel (▶ 30), Musées d'Art Ancien et Moderne (▶ 32, 33), Cathédrale St Michel et Ste Gudule (▶ 36)

Top: interior of the Palais du Roi. Right: Godefroid de Bouillon and the church of St Jacques-sur-Coudenberg

❝ *This elegant, symmetrical neo-classical square has maintained its dignity and is surrounded by some of Belgium's most powerful institutions: the Royal Palace, the Palais de la Nation and the Law Courts.* **❞**

The place Royale The place Royale was built in 1774–80 and was originally an enclosed rectangle with eight palaces joined by porticoes. The Palace of Charles de Lorraine (1766) is the lovely neo-classical building just off the square, under which the Museum of Modern Art has been built.

The square was later opened up with the rue de la Régence on one side, the rue Royale and the park on the other. In its centre stands the statue of Godefroid de Bouillon, who led the first Crusade. The palaces are mostly public offices and the Museums of Classical Art and Modern Art and the Dynasty Museum (1). On the east is the Eglise de St Jacques-sur-Coudenberg (2).

Palais du Roi and parc de Bruxelles Just off the place Royale is the place des Palais with the parc de Bruxelles in its centre. The Palais du Roi (3) is the King's official residence. Along the rue Royale is the Horta-designed Palais des Beaux-Arts (1928) and the Film Museum, and in the rue de la Loi/ Wetstraat the Belgian Parliament, the Palais de la Nation. The park, the former royal hunting grounds, was designed around 1775 by Guimard with several tree-lined avenues leading up to the main fountain.

AVENUE LOUISE

"Once a show-piece of Belgian progress, avenue Louise is now one of the places to go to see ladies heading for the designer boutiques jostle with kids from the fast-food joints."

Imperial design If you have been in Brussels for a few days your eyes will be well-enough adjusted to see that avenue Louise bears the imperial stamp of Leopold II, just as it carries his eldest daughter's name. The avenue was laid out in 1864. Stretching for 2km, as wide as a Parisian boulevard and just about pencil-straight (apart from swerving to avoid the Abbaye de la Cambre, ► 52), it still links central Brussels with the Bois de la Cambre and the countryside beyond.

Shopping Although many Bruxellois turn up their noses at the mention of avenue Louise, it is still one of the shopping streets in the city, lined with big-name designer boutiques, show rooms for interior designers, art galleries, hotels and restaurants. Near place Louise, not far from Leopold's Palais de Justice, café-lined alleys run off the avenue. Beyond place Stéphanieplein, the avenue widens, the buildings get higher, the lanes of traffic increase and prices in the shops reach for the sky. After that it's time to head for the galleries, the most famous and interesting of which are the Galeries de la Toison d'Or and Galerie Louise, in the avenue de la Toison d'Or.

Horta here At No 224, the architect Horta designed another of his art-nouveau master-pieces, the Hôtel Solvay (1894–98), for which he also designed the furniture and silverware. Rue du Bailli/Baljuwstraat, off the avenue, leads to rue Américaine/Amerikaanse Straat and the Horta Museum (► 31).

HIGHLIGHTS

- Hôtel Solvay
- Chanel and other boutiques
- Galeries de la Toison d'Or
- Abbaye de la Cambre
- Isy Brachot gallery
- Refreshments at Nihoul (No 300, 648 3796)

INFORMATION

- ✚ E8, F9–F10, G10
- ✉ Area around avenue Louise/Louizalaan
- 🍴 Various restaurants and tea rooms
- Ⓜ Louise/Louiza
- 🚋 Tram 91, 92, 93, 94; bus 34, 54, 60
- ♿ Good
- ↔ Les Marolles (► 26), Le Sablon/Zavel (► 30), Palais de Justice/Justitiepaleis (► 54)

Top: window shopping in the avenue Louise

13

CATHÉDRALE ST MICHEL ET STE GUDULE

HIGHLIGHTS

- Stained-glass windows
- 17th-century tapestries by Van der Borght
- Nave pillars representing the 12 apostles
- Baroque pulpit by Henri Verbruggen (1699)
- Tombs of Johann of Brabant and his wife Margaret of York
- Stained glass by a pupil of Rubens in the Chapel of Our Lady of Redemption

INFORMATION

- F7
- Place St Gudule/St Goedele-straat
- 217 8345
- Apr–Oct: Mon–Fri 7–7, Sat 7:30–7, Sun 8–7; Nov–Mar: Mon–Fri 7–6, Sat 7:30–6, Sun 8–6
- None
- Gare Centrale/Centraal Station or Parc/Park
- Few
- Free, entrance to crypt cheap
- Grand'Place (➤ 28), place Royale (➤ 34), Belgian Comic Strip Centre (➤ 37), Museums of Classical and Modern Art (➤ 32, 33), Film Museum (➤ 82)
- Services: in Flemish Sat 4PM; in French Sat 5:30PM, Sun 10, 11:30, 12:30

Top: one of the stained-glass windows in the cathedral's nave

"On a hill between the upper and lower parts of the city, the Cathedral of St Michael and Ste Gudule, with its mixture of styles and influences, expresses the city's ability to compromise and is a fitting venue for grand state occasions."

Growing power During the 12th and 13th centuries, a valuable trade route between Brussels and Germany began to develop. As a result of the city's new wealth, a cathedral was planned which, although not completed until the early 16th century, has fulfilled the ambition of its founders and given the city one of its finest buildings, despite now being surrounded by busy roads and modern developments.

Slow start The cathedral is a mixture of middle and late Gothic styles. The earlier Romano-Gothic elements (particularly the ambulatory and choir) fit happily with those from the Late Gothic period (nave and west façade). The result is a building 108m long by 50m wide, with twin 69m-high towers. It has often been added to and embellished. The latest restorations (since 1983) have exposed elements of an earlier Romanesque church (founded 1047) on which the cathedral was built. The original crypt in particular is worth a visit.

Dedications Although it is known as St Michael's and Ste Gudule's, after Brussels' patron saints, the cathedral was officially dedicated only to St Michael. A story is told that when the building was being dedicated, the authorities in Rome admitted to knowing nothing about Gudule, a local girl turned saint. Her name was therefore officially left off the cathedral, but has since been firmly put back by popular support.

CENTRE BELGE DE LA BANDE DESSINÉE

❝Captain Haddock: 'Land Ho! Land Ho! Thundering typhoons! Land … about time, too!' Tintin: 'Why? … Are we out of fuel-oil?' Haddock: 'Worse than that! … We're out of whisky!!' (Hergé's The Adventures of Tintin – The Shooting Star*)❞*

Comic strips and more comic strips This is one of Brussels' unusual delights, combining comic strips and art nouveau. Comic strips, or *bds* (*bandes dessinées*), were not invented in Belgium, but Belgian artists took the form to new heights. The most famous of them is Hergé (Georges Rémi), whose 1929 creations Tintin and Milou (Snowy) are household names around the world.

Hands-on entertainment The museum is on several floors. The mezzanine houses an extensive archive, a cinema and an exhibition which explains how *bds* are made. On the first floor, sections are devoted to each of the great Belgian *bd* creators, with pages to admire as well as hands-on exhibits. Back on the ground floor, there is an exhibition of work by Victor Horta.

The Magazins Waucquez Monsieur Waucquez commissioned Victor Horta, the master of art nouveau, to build a shop for his fabrics, which opened in 1906 with plant-motif iron-work, a sweeping staircase and glass skylight. Magazins Waucquez closed in 1970 and the building, like many others in central Brussels, was earmarked for demolition but thanks to a pressure group and royal support, the old shop was saved and turned into a museum.

DID YOU KNOW?

- Tintin books have been translated into 51 languages
- More than 200 million Tintin books have been sold worldwide
- Brussels has a Comic Strip Frescoes Route, with the most famous characters painted on façades in the centre of Brussels (map available from Tourist Office on Grand'Place)

INFORMATION

- ✚ F7
- ✉ 20 rue des Sables/Zandstraat
- ☎ 219 1980
- ◔ Tue–Sun 10–6; closed Mon, 1 Jan, 1 & 11 Nov, 25 Dec
- 🍴 Restaurant (£–££)
- Ⓜ Botanique/Botaniek, Gare Centrale/Centraal station, Rogier/de Brouckère
- ▣ Tram 23, 52, 55, 56, 81, 90, 92, 93, 94; bus 38, 58, 61
- ♿ Good
- 💷 Expensive
- ↔ Grand'Place (➤ 28), St Michael's and St Gudule's Cathedral (➤ 36)
- ❓ Reading room Tue–Thu 12–5, Fri 12–6, Sat–Sun 10–6, included in entrance; library same hours, ticket moderate

Left: Tintin's moon rocket

37

PARC DU CINQUANTENAIRE

Top: Autoworld. Above: the Arc de Triomphe

" *The park, built to celebrate 50 years of Belgian independence, has all that you would imagine in the way of grand buildings – even its own Arc de Triomphe. It also has some surprises in store.* **"**

HIGHLIGHTS

- Vintage cars in Autoworld
- Arc de Triomphe
- Lace collection in Royal Museum of Art and History

INFORMATION

➕ H7–8

✉ Main entrances rue de la Loi/Wetstraat & avenue de Tervueren

☎ (1) 736 4165; (2) 733 44 93; (3) 741 7211

🕐 (1) Apr–Oct 10–6, Nov–Mar 10–5 (2) Tue–Sun 9–12, 1–4:45 (3) Tue–Fri 9:30–5, Sat, Sun, holidays10–5

🍴 (1) Café-restaurant (£–££) (2) Cafeteria (£)

Ⓜ Mérode, Schuman

🚌 Tram 81, 82; bus 20, 28, 36, 61, 67, 80

♿ (1) Good (2) few (3) few

💶 (1) Moderate (2) free (3) moderate

The most famous city park In 1880, as part of the celebrations for the 50th anniversary of Belgian Independence, Leopold II ordered the building of two huge halls to hold the National Exhibition, which now house Autoworld and the Aviation Museum, in the Parc du Cinquantenaire/Jubelpark. For the next 25 years the king dreamed about erecting an Arc de Triomphe, which was finally built in 1905 by Charles Girault, architect of the Petit Palais in Paris. In 1918 two colonnades were added, decorated with mosaics glorifying Belgium.

The park has several remarkable monuments, reminders of important international fairs. The Arab-inspired building, which housed a painted panorama of Cairo in the 1897 fair, was converted into Brussels' Grand Mosque in 1977. The small pavilion erected by Victor Horta to house the haut-relief of the Human Passions, by the sculptor Jef Lambeaux, is now closed.

Grand but dusty museums One of the world's most prestigious collections of vintage cars from 1886 up to the 1970s is on show in Autoworld (1). The Royal Museum of the Army and Military History (2) incorporates the Aviation Museum, and houses armour and weapons from medieval times to the present as well as aircraft. The very rich Royal Museum of Art and History (3) has antiquities, a section on non-European civilisations, Belgian archaeological discoveries and an important section devoted to a collection of European decorative arts.

DE VESTEN EN POORTEN

"To understand Bruges' layout, take a ride or walk around its walls, especially the east side, where the gates, ramparts, windmills and canals give the impression of containing the city, as they have done for 600 years."

Fortified Bruges Bruges' original fortifications date back to the first millennium, but nothing survives of the six original bastion gates beyond an inscription on Blinde Ezelstraat marking the location of the South Gate. New defences built to protect the increasingly wealthy medieval city between 1297 and 1300 included seven new gates. The four that survive are: in the east, Kruispoort (Cross Gate, 1402), with a draw-bridge, and Gentpoort (Ghent Gate, 14th century) with twin towers; and, in the west, Smedenpoort (Blacksmiths' Gate, 14th century), Bruges' only two-way gate, and Ezelpoort (Donkeys' Gate, entirely rebuilt in the 17th–18th century).

Blowing in the wind The ramparts that linked the gates on the east side were used as raised platforms for windmills. There were 25 mills marked on a panorama of Bruges in 1562, but today only 3 stand along the canal between Kruispoort and Dampoort and none are from that date. From Kruispoort, the first mill, 'Bonne Chiere' (Good Show), built in 1888 and reconstructed in 1911, has never worked. The third mill, 'De Nieuwe Papegaai' (New Parrot), a 1790 oil mill, was moved to Bruges from Beveren in 1970. The middle mill, 'Sint-Janshuysmolen' (Saint John's House Mill), near the junction of Kruisvest and Roiweg, was built where it stands by bakers in 1770 (open 1 May–30 September, ► 55). A fourth mill, newly constructed, is near the Dampoort.

DID YOU KNOW?

- Stone statue of Saint Adrian (1448, remodelled 1956) on Gentpoort was originally carved by Jan van Cutsegem to ward off plague
- Smedenpoort's bronze skull (hung there in 1911) replaces the real skull of a traitor
- Of the 25 windmills known to have stood in Bruges in 1562, 23 still existed in the 19th century. Between 1863 and 1879, 20 of them were pulled down
- The 7km-long ramparts of Bruges were laid out as parks in the 19th century, making a pleasant walk. The areas around Begijnenvest, Buiten Smedenvest and Kruisvest are among the most beautiful

Top: the Minnewater. Below: the Gentpoort

17

Kathedraal St Salvator

HIGHLIGHTS

- Martyr's Death of Saint Hippolytus, Dirk Bouts' triptych (1470–5)
- Last Supper, Pieter Pourbus
- 14th-century Tanner's Panel
- The Mother of Sorrows
- Baroque statue of God the Father
- Eekhoute Cross in shoemakers' chapel
- 8 tapestries by Jaspar van der Borght

INFORMATION

- ✚ blll
- ✉ Zuidzandstraat
- 🕐 Mon–Fri 2–5, Sun 3–5, closed Sat
- ▢ 1, 2, 3, 4, 5, 8, 9, 11, 13, 16
- ♿ Very good
- 💷 Cathedral free, museum cheap
- ↔ Onze-Lieve-Vrouwekerk (➤43), Gruuthuse Museum (➤44), Markt (➤46)
- ❓ Important concerts and church services for national holidays, check with tourist office

"The cathedral, together with the belfry and the Onze-Lieve-Vrouwekerk, towers above Bruges. Inside, a collection of extraordinary works of art is a reminder of its long and eventful history."

The cathedral A house of prayer existed in this location as early as the 9th century, dedicated to Saint Saviour and Saint Eloi, who is believed to have founded an earlier wooden church here in 660. The oldest sections of the remarkable tower date back to 1127. Towards the end of the 13th century a new cathedral was built. The cathedral was damaged by fires on several occasions and in 1798 many of its riches were stolen by the French, who put the building and its contents up for auction the following year. Happily the citizens were able to buy them back. The neo-Romanesque top was added to the tower in 1844–6 and the spire in 1871.

Sculptures and tapestries The cathedral houses some splendid sculptures and wonderful church furniture. The large statue of God the Father (1682) by Arthur Quellinus is one of the best baroque sculptures in Bruges. The doors of the chapel of the shoemakers' corporation and the sculptures in the Cross chapel and the Peter and Paul Chapel are superb examples of late Gothic oak carving. Six of the eight 18th-century tapestries in the choir and transept, illustrating the life of Christ, were woven in Brussels.

Flemish art in the Museum The Museum displays most of the church's collection. Several of the 120 paintings are superb examples of Flemish art, and there are gold and silver objects, pottery and manuscripts. The *Memorial Plaque of Princess Gunhilde* is one of the oldest proofs of historical ties between Bruges and England.

Top: one of the Brussels tapestries in the cathedral

BEGIJNHOF

❝*Entering across a pretty bridge, visitors come to a world where time has stood still. Though there are no longer any* beguines, *this peaceful oasis begs for silence, slowing down and coming to a rest.*❞

The *beguinage* Many Flemish cities have kept their *beguinages*, but the one in Bruges is undoubtedly one of the oldest and most picturesque. Its origins are somewhat mysterious, but from the 13th century pious women started to live in this community, under the control of a grand lady, cut off from the rest of the city. The Bruges *beguinage* is a closed court (the entrances are shut at night) with houses around a square. Since 1927 it has been occupied by Benedictine nuns, whose severe black and white clothes are a reminder of the habit of the *beguines*. Several times a day they walk through the green garden to the church. The square is particularly beautiful in early spring, when it is covered in daffodils.

The church The simple church (1605) is dedicated, as in many other *beguinages*, to Saint Elisabeth of Hungary, whose portrait hangs above the entrance door. She also appears in a painting by the Bruges master Lodewijk de Deyster (1656–1711). The most important work is the statue of Our Lady of Spermalie from *c*1240, the oldest statue of Our Lady in Bruges. On the left wall is another superb statue of Our Lady of Good Will. The remarkable alabaster sculpture of the Lamentation of Christ at the High Altar dates from the early 17th century.

A *beguine's* **house** This tiny museum, a reconstruction of a 17th-century *beguine's* house with furniture and household goods, gives an idea of how the community used to live.

Our Lady of Good Will

HIGHLIGHTS

- The square
- Statue of Our Lady of Spermalie
- *Beguine's* house

INFORMATION

- ✚ blV
- ✉ Wijngaardplein
- ☎ 33 00 11
- 🕐 Church and *beguinage*: 6–12, 2:30–6; *beguine's* house Dec–Feb: Wed, Thu, Sat, Sun 2:45–4:15, Fri 1:45–6; Mar, Oct, Nov: 10:30–12, 1:45–5; Apr–Sep Mon–Sat 10–12, 1:45–5:30, Sun to 6. Closed Fri mornings
- 🚌 1, 2
- ♿ Good
- 💷 Free, entrance to museum cheap
- ↔ Memling Museum (▶ 42)

ST JANS HOSPITAAL EN MEMLING MUSEUM

DID YOU KNOW?

- On the back of *The Mystical Marriage of St Catherine*, Memling has painted the donors
- Jan Florein donated *The Adoration of the Magi*, and is shown kneeling on the left of the painting
- Adriaan Reins, friar of the hospital, is on the side panel of *The Lamentation of Christ*
- Maria Portal floodlit

INFORMATION

- ✚ blV
- ✉ Mariastraat 38
- ☎ 44 87 11
- 🕐 1 Apr–30 Sep, daily 9:30–5; 1 Oct–31 Mar, 9:30–12:30, 2–5. Closed Wed
- 🍴 Several near by
- ♿ Very good
- 💷 Moderate
- ↔ Canals (► 59)

Madonna with apple, *Memling 1487*

❝Among the 'must-sees' of Bruges are the Memling works on show here, landmarks in the history of painting. It's a bonus that the building which houses them is also a gem. Not to be missed.❞

The Hospital St John's, founded in the 12th century, is one of Europe's oldest hospices and was functioning as a hospital until 1976, when medical care was moved to a new building. The Gothic Maria Portal (*c* 1270) on Mariastraat is the original gate to the hospital. Subsequent buildings included a tower, central ward, monastery, brewery, bath-house and cemetery (14th century), St Cornelius Chapel (mid-15th century) and a convent for the hospital's sisters (1539). The old wards are used to display paintings and objects related to the hospital's history. The 17th-century dispensary, with its ancient remedies, is particularly interesting.

The Memling masterpieces As St John's reputation as a hospital grew so its wealth increased. Its funds were invested, with inspiration, in the works of Hans Memling, a German painter who had settled in Bruges by 1465 and died there, one of its richest citizens, in 1494. Four of the six works on show here were commissioned by friars and sisters of the hospice, the most famous and unusual being the *Ursula Shrine* (1489), a relic box in the shape of a church, gilded and painted with scenes from the life of St Ursula. The *Mystical Marriage of St Catherine* (1479), a triptych, was commissioned for the chapel's main altar, as were two smaller triptychs – *The Adoration of the Magi* (1479) and The *Lamentation of Christ* (1480). The diptych *Madonna with Child* (1487) and the portrait of *The Sibylla Sambetha* (1480) were both moved here from the former St Julian's hospice in 1815.

ONZE-LIEVE-VROUWEKERK

"A monumental brick tower draws the curious visitor towards the church. Inside, you enter a world where religious piety is mixed with incense, magnificent sculptures and paintings."

One of Bruges' seven wonders Although there was a chapel here about 1,000 years ago, the choir and façade on Mariastraat date to the 13th century, and the aisles and superbly restored Paradise Porch date from the 14th–15th century. The church's most striking feature is the 122m-high tower, begun in the 13th century. Its 45m spire (1440) makes it one of Europe's highest brick buildings.

The star attraction is the *Madonna and Child* by Michelangelo (1475–1564). Other sculptures include a rococo pulpit (1743) designed by the Bruges painter Jan Garemijn, some fine altars and the Lanchals monument in the Lanchals chapel. The prayer balcony connected to the Gruuthuse (▶ 44) enabled the lords to attend services directly from home. The church contains some important Flemish paintings, including works by Gerard David, Pieter Pourbus and Adriaan Isenbrandt. The valuable *Katte of Beversluys*, kept in the sacristy, weighs 3kg and is embellished with enamel and precious stones.

Mausoleums Both Charles the Bold (d. 1477) and Mary of Burgundy who died in 1482, after a hunting fall, are buried here in superb mausoleums, next to each other. In 1806 they were moved to the Lanchals chapel, but returned in 1979 to their original place in the presbytery. Excavations revealed beautiful frescoes in other tombs and also the fact that Mary's skeleton was buried with the heart of her son Philip the Fair.

HIGHLIGHTS

- Brick tower
- Paradise Porch
- Mausoleums of Charles the Bold and Mary of Burgundy
- *Madonna and Child*, Michaelangelo
- *The Adoration of the Shepherds*, Pieter Poubus
- *Our Lady of the Seven Sorrows*, probably by Isenbrandt
- *The Transfiguration of Mount Tabor*, Gerard David

INFORMATION

- ✠ blV
- ✉ Mariastraat
- 🕐 Mon–Sat 10–11:30, 2:30–5, Sun 2:30–5. On Sat, mausoleums are open 10–11:30, 2:30–4:30. In winter, the church is open until 4:30, the mausoleums until 4
- 🚪 1
- ♿ Very good
- 💶 Church free, mausoleums cheap
- 🔗 St Salvator's Kathedraal (▶ 40), Begijnhof (▶ 41), Memling Museum (▶ 42), Gruuthuse Museum (▶ 44), Groeninge Museum (▶ 45)
- ❓ Weekend services Sat 5 & 6:30PM, Sun 11AM

Top: mausoleum of Charles the Bold

21

GRUUTHUSE MUSEUM

HIGHLIGHTS

- Sculpture rooms
- Guillotine and 15th-century statue of Saint Sebastian
- Prayer balcony
- Gombault and Macée Tapestry series
- Lace collection
- Illuminated courtyard at night
- Smallest window in Bruges, seen from the Boniface Bridge
- Views from loggia over Reie, Boniface Bridge and Onze-Lieve-Vrouwekerk

INFORMATION

- ✚ bIII
- ✉ Dijver 17
- ☎ 44 87 62; Brangwyn Museum 44 87 63
- 🕓 Apr–Sep: daily 9:30–5; Oct–Mar: Wed–Mon 9:30–12:30, 2–5. Closed Tue Brangwyn Museum: same opening times
- 🚌 1
- ♿ None
- 💰 Moderate, Brangwyn Museum cheap
- ↔ Kathedraal St Salvator (► 40), St Jans Hospitaal en Memling Museum (► 42), Onze-Lieve-Vrouwekerk (► 43), Groeninge Museum (► 45)

Top: A delicate ironwork sign outside refers to the brewhouse origins of the palace

❝ *The peaceful courtyard and façade of the Gruuthuse Palace belong to another era. Strolling around the Arentspark and watching the boats pass under the Boniface Bridge, one of Bruges most romantic corners, are a delight.* **❞**

The palace of Gruuthuse The Gruuthuse Palace, built in the late 15th century by the humanist and arts lover Louis van Gruuthuse, now houses the Municipal Museum for Archaeology and Applied Arts. Rooms 5–7 are dedicated to sculptures including a Gothic oak sculpture of the Kneeling Angel (early 16th century), the impressive *Christ, Man of Sorrows* (c1500) and the *Reading Madonna* by Adriaan van Wezel (15th century). Room 22 has an important collection of armoury, instruments of torture and a guillotine which was once used in Bruges.

Tapestries The well-preserved Brugean tapestries (17th century) in the Tapestry Room represent the Seven Liberal Arts, while some fine baroque wool and silk tapestries in Room 8 have pastoral themes, including the *Country Meal*, part of the Gombault and Macée series. There is also a collection of lace. Room 16 is the prayer room or balcony which looks down into the Onze-Lieve-Vrouwekerk (► 43). Together with the kitchen, it is the oldest part of the house.

Brangwyn Museum (Arents Huis) The neighbouring Arents Huis houses four important donations to Bruges. A pewter-ware collection from the 18th–20th centuries, 18th and 19th-century works of art including some exquisite china, a collection of mother-of-pearl, and the world's largest collection of paintings by Frank Brangwyn (1867–1956), a British painter born in Bruges, who studied under William Morris.

GROENINGE MUSEUM

"*The skinning alive of Judge Sisammes, in* The Judgement of Cambyses *by Gerard David, and Van Eyck's portrait of his wife remain so vividly in the mind that the collection of contemporary art is easily overlooked.***"**

The Flemish Primitives The 15th-century Flemish Primitives were so named in the 19th century to express a yearning for medieval purity. Room 1 shows works by Jan Van Eyck (*c*1390–1441), including the *Madonna with Canon Joris van der Paele* and the superb *Portrait of Margaretha Van Eyck*, the painter's wife. Two important works by Memling – The *Moreel Triptych* and two panels of *The Annunciation* – are here. Other masters displayed here include Rogier Van der Weyden and Hugo van der Goes, and the last of the Flemish Primitives, Gerard David, with such works as *The Judgement of Cambyses* and the large triptych *The Baptism of Christ*. In Room 7 the 16th-century works of Pieter Pourbus show an Italian influence on Flemish style. In Room 8 look out for Jacob van Oost's (1601–71) lovely baroque *Portrait of a Brugean Family*.

Modern Flemish masters Emile Claus (1849–1924), Flemish impressionist, and Rik Wouters are well represented. Also worth looking for are James Ensor's *Le Parc aux oiselles*, Gust de Smet, Gustave van de Woestijne, Rik Slabbinck and most of all work by Constant Permeke, some of the best of Flemish expressionism. There are two paintings by Paul Delvaux and one by René Magritte. The last room is dedicated to more recent works by Brugeans Luc Peire and Gilbert Swimberghe, work by Roger Raveel and a cabinet by Marcel Broodthaers (1924–75).

HIGHLIGHTS

- *Death of Our Lady,* Hugo van der Goes
- *Moreel Triptych,* Hans Memling
- *Last Judgement,* Hieronymus Bosch
- *The Angelus* and *The Porridge Eater,* Constant Permeke

INFORMATION

- ✚ dlll
- ✉ Dijver 12
- ☎ 44 87 50
- 🕐 Apr–Sep: daily 9:30–5; Oct–Mar: 9:30–12:30, 2–5; closed Tue
- 🍴 Cafeteria (£)
- ▣ 1
- ♿ Good
- ▣ Expensive
- ↔ Markt (► 46), canals (► 59)

Top: Portrait of a Brugean Family. *Below:* the Moreel Triptych

23

MARKT

"...As the evening shades descended,
Low and loud and sweetly blended,
Low at times and loud at times,
And changing like a poet's rhymes,
Rang the beautiful wild chimes,
From the belfry in the markt
of the ancient tower of Bruges."
(*from* **The Belfry of Bruges** *by Longfellow*)

The historic square A weekly market was held in this square from 1200 onwards until it was moved to 't Zand in 1983. This was where tournaments and pageants took place and where the guillotine and gallows once stood. The neo-Gothic Provincial Government Palace and the Central Post Office (1887–1921) stand on the site of the former Waterhalles, a huge covered dock where ships moored. The oldest façade in the square, the Bouchoute house on the west side (at the corner with the Sint-Amandstraat), has a wind dial and vane. Maximilian of Austria was locked up in 1488 in Craenenburgh house, across Sint-Amandstraat. The north side was once tilers' and fishmongers' guildhouses. In the middle of the square stands the bronze statue of two medieval Brugean heroes Jan Breydel and Pieter de Coninck (► 12), who led the Brugse Metten and fought in the Battle of the Golden Spurs in 1302.

The Halles and Belfry The origins of the Halles and the Belfry (called 'Halletoren' in Bruges) go back to the 13th century, when the Halles were originally the seat of the municipality and the city's treasury. From the first-floor balcony, the bailiff read the 'Halles commands', while the bells warned citizens on all kinds of occasions. The Madonna statue (1525) over the entrance is by Lancelot Blondeel.

BURG

> **Feel the grandeur of times past on the Burg, a place more evocative of medieval Bruges than anywhere else in the city. The impressive façades of this historic enclave once contained the offices of the city, count, church and judicial authorities.**

A **separate entity** Until the 18th century the Burg was walled in and locked with four gates. The north side of the square was covered by the 10th-century Saint Donatian's Church, sold by auction and torn down soon after in 1799. There is a scale model of the church under the trees, while some of its foundations can be seen in the basement of the Holiday Inn Hotel.

The whole of the west side was once the impressive Steen, an 11th-century tower of which only the porch building beside the stairs to the Basilica of the Holy Blood (➤ 48) remains today. To the left of the Town Hall, across Blinde Ezelstraat, is the Flemish-Renaissance Civil Recorders' House (1535–7). Next door is the Palace (1722–27) of the Brugse Vrije, the rural region along the coast which was subordinate to Bruges. The building was the Palace of Justice until the 1980s, but now houses the tourist office and a museum containing the 'Mantelpiece of Charles V', a Renaissance work of art by Lancelot Blondeel.

The **Town Hall** Built between 1376 and 1420, Bruges' Town Hall is the oldest and one of the most beautiful in Belgium. The statues on its Gothic façade were replaced for the second time in the 1970s, with modern statues. The Gothic Room is where Philip the Good called together the first States General of the Ancient Low Countries in 1464; it is now reserved for civil weddings and receptions.

Above: detail of the Town Hall façade

HIGHLIGHTS

- Gothic Room in the Town Hall
- Town Hall façade
- Mantelpiece of Charles V in Brugse Vrije museum
- Waffles with cream in Tom Pouce tea room

INFORMATION

- ✚ bIII
- ✉ Burg
- ☎ (Tourist Office 44 86 86)
- 🕒 Town Hall (Gothic Room): Apr–Sep: 9:30–5; Oct–Mar: 9:30–12:30, 2–5. Museum Brugse Vrije: all year 10–12, 1:30–5. Closed Mon & Jan
- 🍴 Tea room Tom Pouce (£–££)
- 🚌 All buses to the Markt
- ♿ Very good
- 💷 Cheap
- ↔ Markt (➤ 46), Basilica of the Holy Blood (➤ 48)
- ❓ Concerts in summer

47

BRUGES

HEILIG BLOEDBASILIEK

INFORMATION

- ✚ blll
- ✉ Burg 10
- 🕐 Apr–Sep: daily 9:30–12, 2–6; Oct–Mar: 10–12, 2–4. Closed Wed PM, 1 Jan, 1 Nov, 25 Dec and during services
- 🚌 All buses to the Markt
- ♿ None
- 🍽 Cheap
- ↔ Markt (► 46), Burg (► 47), canals (► 59)
- ❓ Sun services, 8AM–11AM. Worship of the Holy Blood: Fri 8:30–11:45, 3–4; Ascension Day 8:30–10:15 & from 6PM onwards

Top: Heilig Bloedkapel façade. Below: Heilig Bloed Procession, May

"The Romanesque Chapel of the Holy Blood, shrouded in mystery, darkness and devotion, is rich with the atmosphere of the Middle Ages. Even convinced atheists fall silent when faced with the continuing devotion of the people."

The Holy Blood Thierry of Alsace, Count of Flanders and a courageous crusader, is said to have received the relic with the blood of Jesus from the Patriarch of Jerusalem. He brought it to Bruges in 1150. The relic is stored in two crystal vials. Every Friday it is exhibited for adoration on the Blessing Altar in the Chapel of the Holy Blood or the upper church. Although the upper church was Romanesque, it has been heavily restored in clumsy Gothic style. The original 15th-century stained-glass windows are now in London's Victoria & Albert Museum. The ones here are 19th-century copies.

The museum contains paintings, silverware, tapestries and the Reliquary of the Holy Blood. The gold and silver reliquary (1617) was made by Renaissance goldsmith Jan Crabbe, and is decorated with pearls and precious stones. Each year it is carried around the city in the Procession of the Holy Blood (► 60).

Saint Basil's Chapel (lower church) This small Romanesque three-aisled church supported on thick sandstone columns was built around 1139 by Count Thierry of Alsace. It is dedicated to the Virgin Mary and to Saint Basil, the patron saint of bricklayers. The wooden *Virgin with Child* (c1300) is one of Bruges' most beautiful Gothic statues. The less refined 19th-century *Ecce Homo* in the side chapel is much adored. In the side-chapel passage stands Bruges' oldest sculpture, a low-relief baptism (c1100).

BRUSSELS
& BRUGES'
best

MUSEUMS

Name a famous Belgian

How about Adolphe Sax, the inventor of the saxophone? A few saxophones are on show in the Sax Room of the Musée Instrumental (place du Petit Sablon 17 ☎ 511 3595 🕐 Tue–Fri 9:30–4:45, Sat 10–4:45), one of the world's great collections of musical instruments, soon to move to the stunning Magasins Old England on the place Royale.

Below: Royal Museum for Central Africa

BRUSSELS

See Top 25 Sights for
CENTRE BELGE DE LA BANDE DESSINÉE (▶ 37)
MUSÉE D'ART ANCIEN (▶ 32)
MUSÉE D'ART MODERNE (▶ 33)
MUSÉE DE VICTOR HORTA (▶ 31)
MUSEUMS OF THE PARC DU CINQUANTENAIRE (▶ 38)

BRUSSELS GUEUZE MUSEUM

The family-run Cantillon brewery, founded in 1900 and the last of the 50 independent lambic breweries in Brussels, still produces the beer in exactly the same way with the original equipment.
➕ D7–8 ✉ Brasserie Cantillon, 56 rue Gheudestraat ☎ 521 4928 🕐 Mon–Fri 8:30–4:30; Sat 10–6 (15 Oct–31 May) and Sat 10–1 (1 Jun–14 Oct). Closed Sun and holidays 🚇 Gare du Midi/Zuidstation, Clémenceau 🚋 Tram 18, 23, 52, 55, 56, 81, 82, 90; bus 20,47 ♿ Few 💳 Moderate

COSTUME AND LACE MUSEUM

A fine collection of old lace, embroidery, costumes and fashion, a studio for courses in lace-making and interesting temporary exhibitions.
➕ E7 ✉ 6 rue de la Violette/Violetstraat ☎ 512 77 09 🕐 Apr–Sep: Mon, Tue, Thu, Fri 10–12:30 & 1:30–5; Sat–Sun 2–5:30; Oct–Mar: Mon, Tue, Thu, Fri 10–12:30 & 1:30–4; Sat–Sun 2–4. Closed 1 Jan, 1 May, 1 Nov, 11 Nov, 25 Dec and election days 🚇 Gare Centrale/Centraal Station 🚋 Tram 23, 52, 55, 56, 81 (Bourse/Beurs); bus 29, 34, 38, 47, 48, 60, 63, 65, 66, 71, 95, 96 ♿ Good 💳 Moderate

MUSEUM OF THE CITY OF BRUSSELS

This 19th-century building, a careful reconstruction of the original Maison du Roi, is devoted to the city's history in all aspects, housing a fine collection of paintings, tapestries, maps and manuscripts and the

extensive wardrobe of Manneken Pis (➤ 27).

🔲 E7 ✉ Maison du Roi, Grand'Place ☎ 511 2742 🕐 Apr–Sep: Mon–Thu 10–12:30 & 1:30–5; Sat–Sun 10–1. Oct–Mar: Mon–Thu 10–12:30, 1:30–4; Sat–Sun 10–1. Closed Fri, 1 Jan, 1 May, 1 Nov, 11 Nov, 25 Dec 🚇 Bourse/Beurs, Gare Centrale/Centraal Station 🚊 Tram 23, 52, 55, 56, 81 (Bourse/Beurs); bus 29, 34, 47, 48, 60, 63, 65, 66, 71, 95, 96 ⚿ Few 💷 Moderate

ROYAL MUSEUM FOR CENTRAL AFRICA

When it opened in 1897, the Museum voor Midden-Afrika glorified the Belgian presence in Africa. Now, despite its grand façade, it is a musty place, popular with children for its dioramas with stuffed animals and for its large collection of creepy crawlies.

🔲 Off map ✉ 13 Leuvensesteenweg, Tervuren ☎ 769 5211 🕐 16 Mar–15 Oct: 9–5:30; 16 Oct–15 Mar: 10–4:30. Closed Mon, 1 Jan, 25 Dec 🍴 Cafeteria (£) 🚊 Tram 44 from Montgomery ⚿ Good 💷 Moderate

BRUGES

See Top 25 Sights for
GROENINGE MUSEUM (➤ 45)
GRUUTHUSE MUSEUM (➤ 44)
MEMLING MUSEUM (➤ 42)

MUSEUM ONZE-LIEVE-VROUW TER POTTERIE

A wonderful little museum in a former hospital (13th–17th century), which has been run as a nursing-home since the 15th century. There are sculptures, 15th and 16th-century paintings, tapestries and furniture. The church has one of Bruges' finest baroque interiors.

🔲 cII ✉ Potterierei 79 ☎ 44 87 11 🕐 Apr–Sep: Thu–Tue 9:30–12:30, 1:15–5; Oct–Mar: Thu–Tue 2–5. Closed Wed 🚊 4 ⚿ Very good 💷 Moderate

MUSEUM VOOR VOLKSKUNDE

Bruges' past is recalled in these 17th–century almshouses. Reconstructions of traditional professions, costumes and items of popular worship.

🔲 dII ✉ Rolweg 40 ☎ 44 87 11 🕐 Apr–Sep: daily 9:30–5; Oct–Mar: Wed–Mon; 9:30–12:30, 2–5 🍴 Medieval inn In de Zwarte Kat (£) 🚊 4, 6 ⚿ Good 💷 Moderate

Monsieur Wiertz

'I make paintings for the honour and portraits for the soup' said Antoine Wiertz, who won the Prize of Rome in 1832 and who wanted to be the Belgian Michelangelo. Since he could not paint the Sistine Chapel, he exhibited gigantic Romantic canvases in his atelier, now the Wiertz Museum (✉ 62, rue Vautierstraat ☎ 648 1718 🕐 Tue–Fri 10–12 & 1–5).

Above left: Ter Potterie Museum.
Below: Museum voor Volkskunde

51

CHURCHES

Flat land

'With its cathedrals as only
mountains
And its dark clock towers like
poles of plenty
Where stone devils snatch at
clouds,
With the thread that links the
days as the only journey
And wet roads as the only evening
salute,
With the west wind – listen to the
wanting –
The flat country which is mine..'
(From Jacques Brel's *Le plat pays*)

*Above: Abbaye de la
Cambre. Below: Notre
Dame de la Chapelle,
detail*

BRUSSELS

See Top 25 Sights for
LA BASILIQUE DE KOEKELBERG (➤ 24)
CATHÉDRALE ST MICHEL ET STE GUDULE (➤ 36)
EGLISE NOTRE DAME DU SABLON (➤ 30)
EGLISE ST JACQUES-SUR-COUDENBERG (➤ 34)

ABBAYE DE LA CAMBRE/TER KAMEREN
Founded in 1201 for the Cistercian Order, but exten-
sively rebuilt during the 16th and 18th centuries. A
14th-century church is attached to the abbey, and the
buildings are set in elegant French gardens.
➕ G10 ✉ avenue E Duray ☎ 648 1121 🕐 Mon–Fri 9–12, 3–6;
Sat 3–6; Sun 8–12:30, 3–6; Catholic feast days 9–12 🚋 Tram 23, 90,
94 ♿ Few 💷 Free

COLLEGIATE CHURCH OF SAINTS PIERRE ET
GUIDON
The Romanesque crypt is 11th century, but the
superb Gothic church with frescoes is from the 14th
to 16th centuries. A rare Celtic tombstone is believed
to belong to St Guidon.
➕ B8 ✉ place de la Vaillance/Dapperheidsplein ☎ 521 8415
🕐 Mon–Fri 9–12, 2:30–6. Closed Sun, holiday afternoons and during
services 🚇 St Guidon ♿ Few 💷 Free

ÉGLISE NOTRE-DAME DE LA CHAPELLE/KERK VAN ONZE-LIEVE-VROUW-TER-KAPELLE

This is where Pieter Bruegel the Elder was buried. A memorial was erected by his son.

➕ E8 ✉ 4 rue des Ursulines ☎ 229 1744 🕐 Summer, daily 9–5, Sun 1–3:30; Winter 1–4, Sun 1–3:30 🚇 Gare Centrale/Centraal Station 🚌 Bus 20, 48 ♿ Few 🎫 Free

ÉGLISE NOTRE-DAME DE LAEKEN/KERK VAN ONZE-LIEVE-VROUW-VAN-LAKEN

A massive neo-Gothic church, commissioned by Leopold I and designed by Poelaert in 1851. The burial-place of the Belgian royal family.

➕ E3 ✉ parvis Notre Dame ☎ 478 2095 🕐 Guided tours Sun 2–6; services 1st Fri of the month 5, Sat 5, Sun 9:15, 10:15, 11:30 🚋 Tram 81; bus 53 ♿ Few 🎫 Free

ÉGLISE ST CATHERINE/ST-KATELIJNEKERK

The interior of St Catherine's, built by Poelaert in 1854 over part of the old port, is more attractive than the outside. A tower of the former 17th-century church survives.

➕ E7 ✉ place St Catherine ☎ 513 3481 🕐 Mon–Sat 8–5; Sun 8–12. Closed holidays 🚇 Ste Catherine ♿ Few 🎫 Free

ÉGLISE ST NICOLAS/ST-NIKLAASKERK

Brussels' oldest church was founded in the 11th century, but most of the interior dates from the 18th century. It is curved, as it once followed the line of the River Senne, and a cannon ball in the wall is proof that the church survived the bombardment of 1695.

➕ E7 ✉ 1 rue au Beurre/Boterstraat ☎ 513 8022 🕐 Daily, 7:45–5, Sun 8–5 🚋 Tram 23, 52, 55, 56, 81 (Bourse/Beurs); bus 29, 34, 47, 48, 60, 63, 65, 66, 71, 95, 96 ♿ Good 🎫 Free

BRUGES

**See Top 25 Sights for
HEILIG BLOEDBASILIEK (▶ 48)
KATHEDRAAL ST SALVATOR (▶ 40)
ONZE-LIEVE-VROUWEKERK (▶ 43)**

JERUZALEMKERK

The 15th-century building was inspired by the basilica of the Holy Sepulchre in Jerusalem. Half of the original 12 almshouses attached to the church have survived and are now the Kantcentrum (Lace Centre, ▶ 70).

➕ cIII ✉ Peperstraat 3a ☎ 33 00 72 🕐 Mon–Fri 10–12, 2–6; Sat 10–1, 2–5. Closed Sun and holidays 🚌 4, 6 ♿ Good 🎫 Cheap

SINT-WALBURGAKERK

Splendid baroque church built by the Jesuit Pieter Huyssens between 1619 and 1642, with an astonishing 17th-century oak pulpit.

➕ cIII ✉ Sint-Maartensplein ☎ 34 32 57 🕐 Summer: 8–10PM, occasionally during the day; Winter: only during Sunday services, 10, 7 🚌 6 ♿ None 🎫 Free

---

The Brussels *Béguinage* (Begijnhof)

The church of St John the Baptist, the finest example of Flemish baroque in the country, and the rue du Béguinage/Begijnhofstraat are all that are left of the once flourishing *Béguinage* founded in the 13th century outside the city walls. The former gardens were used to build the Hospice Pachéco, created in 1824 and still in use today. (➕ E6 ✉ .place du Béguinage ☎ 217 8742 🕐 Tue 10–5; Wed–Fri 9–5; first, third, fifth Sat in month 10–5 🚋 Tram 92, 93, 94, bus 58, 61 ♿ Good 🎫 Free)

Jeruzalemkerk

ARCHITECTURE

Famous Brussels residents

Pieter Bruegel was born in the Marolles (▶ 26) and his house at 132 rue Haute has been restored (visits by prior arrangement with written request). Erasmus spent five months in 1521 at 31 rue de Chapitre. Now a museum, it contains an important collection of his and other humanists' documents and Renaissance furniture (☎ 521 1383 ☒ St Guidon).

Art nouveau Old England

BRUSSELS

See Top 25 Sights for
GUILDHOUSES ON THE GRAND'PLACE (▶ 28)
HÔTEL DE VILLE (▶ 29)
HOTEL SOLVAY IN AVENUE LOUISE (▶ 35)
MAGAZINS WAUCQUEZ (▶ 37)
MUSÉE DE VICTOR HORTA (▶ 31)
**MUSEUMS OF THE PARC DU
    CINQUANTENAIRE** (▶ 38)

BOURSE/BEURS

The Belgian Stock Exchange is set in an elegant building with a decorative frieze by Carrier-Belleuse and sculptures by Rodin.
➕ E7 ☒ 2, rue H Maussstraat ☎ 509 1211 ⏰ Mon–Fri only for groups by prior arrangement 🚊 Tram 23, 52, 55, 56, 81 (Bourse/Beurs) ♿ Few 🎟 Free

COLONNE DU CONGRÈS/KONGRESZUIL

Designed by Poelaert, surmounted by a statue of Leopold I, and erected in 1850 to commemorate the National Congress of 1831. At the foot burns the flame for the Unknown Soldiers of both world wars.
➕ F7 ☒ place du Congrès/Kongresplein 🚇 Madou ♿ Good 🎟 Free

PALAIS DE JUSTICE/ JUSTITIEPALEIS

One of Leopold II's pet projects, designed by Poelaert in a grand eclectic style. The interior is equally overwhelming and so are the fine views over Brussels from the terrace.
➕ E8 ☒ place Poelaertplein ☎ 508 6410 ⏰ Mon–Fri 9–12:30, 1:30–4. Closed weekends and holidays 🚇 Louise 🚊 Tram 92, 93, 94 ♿ Very good 🎟 Free

PORTE DE HAL/HALLEPOORT

The gate, completely restored in 1991, with its 14th-century tower, was originally planned as an entrance to the city.
➕ D–E9 ☒ boulevard du Midi/Zuidlaan ☎ 534 2552 ⏰ Tue–Sun 10–5. Closed Mon, 1 Jan, 1 May, 1 Nov, 11 Nov, 25 Dec 🚇 Porte de Hal 🚊 Tram 23, 55, 90; bus 20, 48 ♿ Good 🎟 Moderate

RÉSIDENCE PALACE

This was Brussels' largest and

most luxurious apartment building, in art-deco style, since converted into offices. The sumptuous pool was inspired by the ruins of Pompei.

🟦 G7 ✉ 155 rue de la Loi/Wetstraat ☎ 231 0305 🕔 Open only for events 🚇 Schuman

ROYAL GREENHOUSES (LAEKEN)

Magnificent 'city of glass' built by Balat and the young Horta for Leopold II. Rarely open, but the exterior can be seen from the avenue du Parc Royal.

🟦 F2 ✉ 61 avenue du Parc Royal (Domaine Royal) ☎ 513 8940 (tourist information) 🕔 Open only two weeks a year end of Apr–May when flowers are in bloom. Check with tourist office for exact dates and times 🚇 Heysel/Heizel 🚃 Tram 52, 92; bus 53 ⚱ Few 💶 Free during the day, moderate at night

LA MONNAIE/DE MUNT

The original 1697 theatre, properly known as Théâtre royal de la Monnaie/Koninklijke Muntschouwburg, was enlarged in 1819 by Napoleon to become one of the most beautiful in the world. In 1985 it was again enlarged, with a ceiling by Sam Francis and tiling by Sol Lewitt.

🟦 E7 ✉ 4 rue Léopold/Leopoldstraat ☎ 229 3400, box office ➤ 80 🕔 Tours: Sat 12 noon, French and Flemish only (30 mins) 🚇 De Brouckère ⚱ Very good 💶 Moderate (tour)

BRUGES

SINT-JANSHUYSMOLEN

The only one of the four windmills in Bruges which can be visited, the St Janshuysmolen was built by a group of bakers in 1770 and acquired by the city of Bruges in 1914. It still grinds grain. Inside is a small museum.

🟦 dll ✉ Kruisvest ☎ 44 87 11 🕔 May–Sep 9:30–12:30, 1:15–5 🚃 4, 6,16 ⚱ None 💶 Cheap

Seven Wonders

The *Septem admirationes civitatis Brugensis* (Bruges' Seven Wonders) by P. Claeissins the Elder (1499–1576), in the *Beguinage*, depicts the Onze-Lieve-Vrouwekerk tower, the Halles and belfry, as well as the House with the Seven Turrets, the Water Hall on the Markt, the Water House and the Hansa House, now all disappeared, and the Poorters' Lodge.

Bruges' belfry

ATTRACTIONS FOR CHILDREN

Brussels for children

Despite appearances, Brussels has plenty to offer children. Apart from parks and adventure parks, most activities happen indoors. The Film museum (➤ 82), the Strip Cartoon Museum (➤ 37), the museums of Classical and Modern Art (➤ 32–3) and the Royal Museum for Central Africa (➤ 51) have workshops for children of various ages. Details in *The Bulletin* (➤ 22).

Gaston Lagaffe/Guust Flater

See Top 25 Sights for
AUTOWORLD (➤ 38)
CENTRE BELGE DE LA BANDE DESSINÉE (➤ 37)
ROYAL MUSEUM OF ART AND HISTORY (➤ 38)
**ROYAL MUSEUM OF THE ARMY AND MILITARY
HISTORY (➤ 38)**

BRUPARCK
Bruparck has Mini-Europe – 350 models of monuments in the European community – a launchpad for the Ariane space rocket and the Océade, a tropical beach.
✚ D2 ⊠ boulevard du Centenaire 20, Heysel/Heizel ☎ 477 0377 ◷ Varies with season and attraction; phone first ⅰ Restaurants and cafeterias in The Village ◉ Heysel ♿ Good ⓦ Very expensive

MUSÉE DES ENFANTS/KINDERMUSEUM
For children aged 4 to 12. In Flemish and French only.
✚ G10 ⊠ 15 rue du Bourgmestre/Burgemeesterstraat ☎ 640 0107 ◷ Wed, Sat 2:30–5 ▣ Tram 23, 90, 93, 94; bus 71 ♿ Good ⓦ Expensive

SCIENTASTIC MUSEUM
Above the Bourse/Beurs Metro station, this fun museum offers interactive experiments and displays.
✚ E7 ⊠ Metro station Bourse, 1st floor ☎ 649 8915 ◷ Sat–Sun 2–5:30. School holidays & daily July–Aug 2–5:30; closed mid Dec–mid Jan ◉ Bourse/Beurs ♿ Good ⓦ Moderate

WALIBI
Theme parks with breathtaking adventures, and play area for smaller children.
✚ Off map ⊠ Motorway E411 Brussels-Namur, exit 6, in Wavres/Waveren ☎ 41 44 66 ◷ May–Aug: 10–6; Sep: Sat–Sun, 10–6 ⅰ Several restaurants and cafés (£–££) ◉ Train from Gare Schuman to Gare de Bierges on Ottignies/Louvain-la-Neuve line (300m walk from station) ♿ Few ⓦ Very expensive

BOUDEWIJNPARK
30 attractions and shows, ice show and Europe's most sophisticated dolphinarium.
✚ Off map ⊠ avenue De Baeckestraat 12, St Michiels ☎ 38 38 38 ◷ May–Aug 10–6; Apr & Sep 11–6. Dolphinarium: Mar–Oct more than one show a day; Nov–Feb 4 o'clock show at weekends and holidays ⅰ Restaurant (£–££) ◉ Bus 7, 17 from the railway station ♿ Good ⓦ Very expensive

PARKS

BRUSSELS

See Top 25 Sights for
PARC DE BRUXELLES (► 34)
PARC DU CINQUANTENAIRE (► 38)

BOIS DE LA CAMBRE/TERKAMERENBOS

Once part of the Forest of Soignes, the Bois was annexed by the city in 1862 and laid out by landscape artist Keilig. Boating, fishing, roller-skating.

➕ G11–12 ☒ Main entrance on avenue Louise ◉ Dawn–dusk 🚋 Tram 93, 94 ♿ Few 💵 Free

FORÊT DE SOIGNES/ZONIËNWOUD

Wonderful beech forest which includes Tervuren Arboretum (☎ 769 2081), Groenendaal Arboretum (☎ 657 0386) and Jean Massart Experimental Garden (☎ 673 8406).

➕ G–H–J–K 13 ☒ Boitsfort/Bosvoorde ☎ 215 1740, les Amis de la Forêt de Soignes ◉ Guided tours at 10:30 on Thu and Sun, information on above phone number 🍴 Restaurant (£££) 🚋 Tram 44 ♿ None 💵 Free

PARC DE LAEKEN

Beyond its attractive lawns lie the Royal Residence and the amazing Royal Greenhouses (► 55).

➕ E2 ☒ Main entrance on boulevard de Smet de Naeyer, Laeken ◉ Dawn–dusk 🚇 Heysel ♿ Few 💵 Free

PARC JOSAPHAT

Sculpture museum, animal reserve, sporting facilities. Free Sunday concerts July and August.

➕ G–H5 ☒ Entrance on avenue des Azalées ◉ Dawn–dusk 🍴 Café (£–££) 🚋 Tram 23 ♿ Few 💵 Free

BRUGES

See Top 25 Sights for
CITY RAMPARTS (► 39)

KONINGIN ASTRIDPARK

Laid out in 18th-century English-country style, with a good children' s playground.

➕ clll ☒ Main entrance Park ◉ Always 🚌 1, 11 ♿ Good 💵 Free

MINNEWATERPARK

On edge of Minnewater (Lake of Love), with sculpture garden and free concerts in summer.

➕ blV ☒ Arsenaalstraat ◉ Always 🍴 Café-restaurant (££) 🚌 All buses to the train station ♿ Good 💵 Free

Parc de Bruxelles

Green spaces

Nearly 14 per cent of Brussels is covered by parks and it has an extremely high ratio of green space per inhabitant (27.7sq m). The parks in the centre, although well laid-out, often have a rather charming unkempt and abandoned feel about them, particularly at weekends, when most people head for the magnificent parks and woods just outside Brussels.

MARKETS IN BRUSSELS

Markets in Bruges

The weekly market on the Zand attracts large crowds every Saturday morning. Goods for sale range from clothes to household products, music and farm-made goat's cheese. On the nearby Beursplein, stalls sell fruit, vegetables and flowers. A smaller food and flower market is held on the Markt (➤ 46) on Wednesday mornings.

ANTIQUES MARKET

The place du Grand Sablon is crowded with antique shops, but at weekends there is a small street market with various collectibles. Don't expect bargains!
➕ E8 ✉ place du Grand Sablon 🕐 Sat 9–6; Sun 9–2 🚋 Tram 91, 92, 93, 94; bus 48 ♿ Few 🎫 Free

EXOTIC MARKET (MARCHÉ DU MIDI)

One of Europe's largest and more colourful markets, with food, clothes, household goods, North African music, pictures, books. The closer it gets to mid-day, the bigger the bargains.
➕ D8 ✉ Near the Gare du Midi 🕐 Sun 7am–1pm 🚉 Gare du Midi 🚋 Tram 23, 52, 55, 56, 81, 82, 90 ♿ Few 🎫 Free

FLOWER MARKET

Small flower and plant market in the Grand'Place. On Sunday mornings there is a little more noise, as every type of bird from canaries and parakeets to ducks, hens and doves are sold in the bird market.
➕ E7 ✉ Grand'Place 🕐 Daily 8am–6pm. Flower market Tue–Sun 8–6. Bird market: Sun 7–2 🚋 Tram 23, 52, 55, 56, 81 (Bourse/Beurs) ♿ Good 🎫 Free

HORSE FAIR

The Brabant Province around Brussels is renowned for its strong quadrupeds, still used as draught horses on many Belgian farms. These beautiful horses and racehorses are sold here after much bargaining.
➕ CD7 ✉ place de la Duchesse de Brabant/Hertogin van Brabantplaats 🕐 Fri 6–12 noon 🚉 Gare de l'Ouest/Weststation 🚋 Bus 63, 89 ♿ Few 🎫 Free

VIEUX MARCHÉ

Sunday is definitely the best day to browse around this great junk market. Arrive early for the bargains.
➕ E8 ✉ place du Jeu de Balle/Vossenplein 🕐 Daily 7–2 🚋 Bus 48 ♿ Good 🎫 Free

Sunday morning bird market in the Grand'Place

CANALS IN BRUGES

Bruges is often referred to as 'the Venice of the North' and its *reien* (Flemish for canals) provide much of its romantic charm. Unlike in Venice, the canals are no longer used for public transport, but nevertheless one of the best ways to explore the city centre is to take a boat trip. There are daily guided tours in several languages, except when the canals are frozen. In summer an illuminated evening tour is especially recommended.

AUGUSTIJNENREI
One of the less spectacular canals, but none the less beautiful with the Augustijnen Bridge from *c*1425, and the Spaanse Loskaai, a reminder of the Spanish presence in the 14th and 15th centuries.

 3

Canal along the Dijver

DIJVER
The lovely little walkway along this canal shows some of Bruges' grandest architecture: at No 11 is the College of Europe, No 12 is the Groeninge Museum (► 45), No 17 is the Gruuthuse Museum (► 44). In summer there is a Saturday and Sunday junk market but don't hope for bargains.

1, 6, 11, 16

GROENEREI/STEENHOUWERSDIJK
The view of this canal from the Vismarkt (Fish Market) is one of the most idyllic (and often-painted) in Bruges. The Meebrug and the Peerdenbrug are two of Bruges' oldest stone bridges. At the end of the Groenerei is the almshouse De Pelikaan (1634).

1, 6, 11, 16

ROZENHOEDKAAI
Another wonderful corner, with views of the back of the buildings of the Burg and the Huidenvettersplein and of the famous Duc de Bourgogne Hotel.

1, 6, 11, 16

City of bridges
No name could fit the city better than 'Brugge', Flemish for 'bridge'. The city was apparently at first simply a bridge over the canal (*reie*), probably the Blind Donkey bridge. To protect the crossing, a borough was built and the city gradually grew around that. Bruges still has about 80 bridges, several of which are masterpieces of medieval architecture.

59

FESTIVALS & PROCESSIONS

BRUSSELS

RAISING OF THE MAYPOLE (MEIBOOM)

On 9 August a procession from the Sablon (➤ 30) to the Grand'Place (➤ 28) commemorates an attack on a wedding party in 1213, by bandits from Leuven. The gang was foiled and the grateful duke allowed the party to plant a Meiboom or Maypole on their patron saint's feast day.

OMMEGANG

On the first Tuesday and Thursday in July this colourful procession goes from the place du Grand Sablon (➤ 30) to the Grand'Place (➤ 28). Dating back to the 14th century, it celebrates the arrival

Ommegang *procession*

of a statue of the Virgin from Antwerp. Nowadays it ends in a dance on the illuminated Grand'Place from 9pm to midnight. The expensive tickets need to be booked well in advance.

Tickets and information from the Brussels Tourist Office ⊠ Town Hall Grand'Place, 1000 Brussels ☎ 513 8940 fax: 514 4538

Carnivals

Several Belgian cities, including Bruges and Brussels, celebrate Carnival around mid-February, with a procession and the election of the Carnival Prince. The main event is on Shrove Tuesday, Mardi Gras, when people dressed in richly embroidered costumes and masks dance in the cities' main squares to ward off evil spirits. (Information from the Tourist Offices ➤ 90.)

BRUGES

PAGEANT OF THE GOLDEN TREE (GOUDEN BOOMSTOET)

Magnificent procession, held every five years, re-enacting the festivities for the wedding of Charles the Bold and Margaret of York, celebrated in Bruges in 1468.

PROCESSION OF THE HOLY BLOOD

Every year on Ascension Day (May) at 3pm the golden shrine with the relic of the Holy Blood (➤ 48) is taken out in a spectacular procession involving thousands of participants. As well as scenes from the Bible, referring to medieval passion plays, the legend is told of the coming of the Holy Blood to Bruges and the worship of the relic.

Information: Bruges Tourist Office ⊠ Burg 11 ☎ 448 686

BRUSSELS & BRUGES
where to...

GOURMET BELGIAN

Prices

Expect to pay the following per person for three courses without wine

£££   over 1,500Bf

££   750–1,500Bf

£   under 750Bf

The king of Belgian food

Chef Pierre Wynants, owner and chef of the famous Comme chez Soi restaurant, is an authority on Belgian and European food. He has transformed Belgium's cuisine and has brought traditional ingredients like beer and hop shoots back on the menu. Many have followed his example, so there is a surprising number of good restaurants all over the country.

BRUSSELS

L'ALBAN CHAMBON (£££)

Brilliant French food served perfectly in plush surroundings. House specialities of potatoes with langoustines and truffles, and scallops with truffle vinaigrette are outstanding.

✚ E7 ✉ 31 place de Brouckère plein ☎ 217 7650 ⏰ Lunch, dinner 🚇 De Brouckère 🚊 Tram 23, 52, 55, 56, 81, 90

LA BELLE MARAÎCHÈRE (££–£££)

Traditional and well-known fish restaurant on Brussels' old harbour. The *Waterzooi* with three fishes is excellent and set menus are great value.

✚ E7 ✉ 11 place St Catherine ☎ 512 9759 ⏰ Lunch, dinner. Closed Wed, Thu 🚇 St Catherine 🚊 Tram 23, 52, 55, 56, 81, 90 (Bourse/Beurs)

COMME CHEZ SOI (£££)

By common consent Belgium's finest restaurant (quite something in a country with so many fine restaurants), often fully booked weeks ahead so plenty of planning is essential if you want to indulge in specialities such as sweetbreads with hop shoots or sole fillets with a riesling mousseline and shrimps.

✚ E7 ✉ 23 place Rouppeplein ☎ 512 2921 ⏰ Lunch, dinner. Closed Sun, Mon and 25 Dec–1 Jan & 1–31 Jul 🚇 Anneessens 🚊 Tram 23, 52, 55, 56, 81

L'ECAILLER DU PALAIS ROYALE (£££)

The perfect place to take a Belgian minister or banker. The décor is stuffy and bourgeois, the clientèle serious and respectable, but the food is always impeccable, with excellent croquettes aux crevettes, oysters direct from Zeeland and a wonderful grilled turbot on a coulis of tomatoes. If that isn't enough, succumb to the home-made bitter chocolate ice cream.

✚ E8 ✉ 18 rue Bodenbroeckstraat ☎ 512 8751 ⏰ Lunch and dinner. Closed Sun. Book a week ahead 🚊 Tram 92, 93, 94; bus 34, 95, 96

LA MAISON DU CYGNE (£££)

Heaps of truffles, rich mousses and *foie gras* in this luxurious restaurant with great views of the Grand'Place. Go with an empty stomach and a full wallet.

✚ E7 ✉ 9 Grand'Place ☎ 511 8244 ⏰ Lunch, dinner. Closed Sat lunch, Sun, 25 Dec–1 Jun & 1–21 Aug 🚇 Gare Centrale/Centraal Station

LA MANUFACTURE (££)

Pleasant modern restaurant in the old Delvaux leather factory serving delicious and inventive European food with a touch of Asia, quite rare in Brussels. Courtyard tables in summer.

✚ D7 ✉ 12 rue Notre-Dame du Sommeil ☎ 502 2525 ⏰ Lunch, dinner. Closed Sat lunch & Sun 🚊 Tram 23, 52, 55, 56, 81, 90 (Bourse/Beurs)

LES QUATRE SAISONS (££–£££)

One Michelin star and plenty of praise confirm what you can taste yourself when you try the poached sole with crayfish crème and mushrooms, or salad of lobster and smoked goose liver with balsamic cream. One of Brussels best.

✚ E7 ✉ 5 rue Duquesnoy ☎ 505 5100 🕐 Lunch, dinner. Closed Sat lunch & 20 Jul–17 Aug 🚋 Tram 23, 52, 55, 56, 81, 90 (Bourse/Beurs)

LA TRUFFE NOIR (£££)

Rich black and white truffles with everything in this Italo-French cuisine. An excellent set menu. The *carpaccio* with parmesan flakes and truffle is heavenly.

✚ G10 ✉ 12 boulevard de la Cambre ☎ 640 4422 🕐 Lunch and dinner, closed Sat lunch and Sun 🚋 Tram 23, 90; bus 366

BRUGES

DEN GOUDEN HARYNCK (££–£££)

The Michelin-starred chef prepares the freshest ingredients without too many frills. Specialities include some pleasant surprises like smoked lobster with fig chutney or scallops with goose liver. Typically Brugean décor.

✚ blll1 ✉ Groeninge 25 ☎ 34 42 70 🕐 Lunch, dinner. Closed Sun & Mon 🚌 1

DE KARMELIET (£££)

Often regarded as Bruges' best restaurant, which isn't surprising as it has three Michelin stars. De Karmeliet offers inspired and creative Belgian cuisine, prepared by Geert Van Hecke and served in the stylish high-ceilinged rooms of a mansion house.

✚ dll ✉ Langestraat 19 ☎ 33 82 59 🕐 Mon–Sat lunch & dinner, Sun lunch. Closed Sun eve & Mon

T'PANDREITJE (£££)

Much-lauded restaurant with excellent fish specialities, pariculary a fish pie of smoked eel. There are several *dégustation* menus or à la carte dishes, served in the comfortably plush interior or in the lovely garden in summer.

✚ dll ✉ Pandreitje 6 ☎ 33 11 90 🕐 Lunch, dinner. Closed Sun, Wed 🚌 1, 6, 11, 16

DE SNIPPE (£££)

Popular restaurant in a well-restored 18th-century house. The chef Luc Huysentruyt, a disciple of Escoffier and a Master Chef of Belgium, loves innovation, but his cuisine is strongly rooted in tradition. His specialities are amazing fish dishes.

✚ dll ✉ Nieuwe Gentweg 53 ☎ 33 70 70 🕐 Tue–Sat lunch, dinner, Mon dinner. Closed all day Sun & Mon lunch 🚌 1, 11

DE WITTE POORTE (£££)

Renowned for its gourmet Belgian cuisine in the warm atmosphere of a large room under rustic medieval vaults.

✚ blll ✉ Jan van Eyck Plein 6 ☎ 33 08 83 🕐 Lunch, dinner. Closed Mon & Sat 🚌 4

Everybody eats well in Belgium

To prepare Belgian food yourself read: Ruth Van Waerebeek's beautiful *Everybody Eats Well in Belgium*; Enid and Shirley Gordon's *Belgian Cookbook* with all the Belgian specialities; John Hellon's *Brussels Fare*, a journalist's selection of recipes from the best restaurants; Nika Hezelton's *Belgian Cookbook*; and last but not least *Creative Belgian Cuisine* by the master, Pierre Wynants.

GOOD BELGIAN (BRASSERIES, FRITERIES...)

Poetic mussels

O beautiful city of Brussels
With your parks and statues &
bôites
Where they really know how to
cook mussels...

From W H Auden, *Ode to the New Year*

BRUSSELS

L'ACHEPOT (£–££)

Popular, casual place where real Brussels cuisine is served – offal dishes are the speciality: sweetbreads, brains, veal kidneys and liver.

✚ E7 ✉ 1 place St Catherine ☎ 511 6221 ⏰ Lunch, dinner. Closed Sun ⬛ St Catherine or Bourse

AU STEKERLAPATTE (£)

Long menu of traditional Belgian dishes served in a dark maze of a restaurant. Try the *poularde de Bruxelles au champignons* and the excellent steak tartare. With friendly service and a good atmosphere (it's usually full), this is the place other restaurateurs come on their day off. Recommended.

✚ E8 ✉ 4 rue des Prêtres ☎ 512 8681 ⏰ Dinner 7–1. Closed Mon ⬛ Hôtel des Monnaies/Munthof

CHEZ LEON (££)

The most famous of all Belgian mussels restaurants with paper tablecloths, fast service and large portions of mussels, well prepared, in many different ways.

✚ E7 ✉ 18 rue des Bouchers/Beenhouwersstraat ☎ 511 1415 ⏰ Daily, noon–11PM ⬛ Bourse/Beurs

LE PAIN QUOTIDIEN/HET DAGELIJKS BROOD (£)

Chain of tea rooms where breakfast, lunch, snacks and afternoon tea are served around one big table. The big old-fashioned breads, great pastries and jams are all home made.

✚ E8 ✉ 11 rue des Sablons/Zavelstraat ☎ 513 5154 ⏰ Mon–Sat 7:30–7, Sun 8–7 ⬛ Tram 20, 48; bus 34, 95 (also on 16 Rue Antoine Dansaert Straat ☎ 502 2361 and in Bruges: Philip Stockstraat 21 ☎ 33 60 50, 33 67 66)

MARTENS (££)

This stylish and trendy bare-brick brasserie in the fashionable area of the Dansaertstraat serves light, modern French-Belgian cooking. A popular lunchtime place, with some excellent and very good-value set menus.

✚ E7 ✉ 28 rue Antoine Dansaertstraat ☎ 511 0631 ⏰ Lunch, dinner. Closed Sun–Mon ⬛ Bourse/Beurs

TAVERNE DU PASSAGE (£–££)

This classic and elegant brasserie, which has been here since 1928, certainly does not show its age. It is a charming place renowned for its *croquettes au crevettes* and ultra-traditional Brussels cuisine. The *choucroute au jambonneau* is a recommended speciality.

✚ E7 ✉ 30 Galerie de la Reine/Koninginnegallerij ☎ 512 37 31 ⏰ Daily noon–midnight ⬛ Gare Centrale/Centraal Station

DE ULTIEME HALLUCINATIE (££)

Worth a visit just for the splendid art-nouveau interior, and the French-inspired food also lives up to expectation. Delicious goose- and duck-liver specialities or poached fish in a gueuze sauce. Popular café section.

➕ F6 ✉ 316 rue Royale ☎ 217 0614 🕐 Mon–Fri 11AM–2AM, Sat 5PM–3AM. Closed Sun 🚇 Botanique

VINCENT (££)

Off the busy rue des Bouchers and consequently less touristy, this beautifully tiled brasserie serves traditional Brussels cuisine like mussels and *carbonnades*. As you walk through the steaming kitchen to reach your table, with ingredients hanging from the window, there are no surprises here.

➕ E7 ✉ 8–10 rue des Dominicains ☎ 502 3693 🕐 Lunch, dinner 🚇 Bourse/Beurs

BRUGES

CHEZ OLIVIER (££)

Cosy restaurant in an old house, with views over one of the prettiest canals, serving simple but stylish French fare.

➕ clll ✉ Meestraat 9 ☎ 33 36 59 🕐 Lunch, dinner. Closed Thu, Fri lunch 🚌 6, 16

BREYDEL DE CONINCK (£)

Popular mussel restaurant regarded as the best by many locals, even though the décor is rather dull.

➕ blll ✉ Breidelstraat 24 ☎ 33 97 46 🕐 Lunch, dinner. Closed Wed and all of Jun 🚌 1, 3, 4, 6, 8, 11, 13, 16

DEN DIJVER (££)

All dishes here, be it meat or fish, are lovingly prepared with some kind of Belgian beer. The interior is old-Flemish, while the view from the terrace in summer is one of the best in town.

➕ blll ✉ Dijver 5 ☎ 33 60 69 🕐 Lunch, dinner. Closed Wed (&Tue in winter) 🚌 1, 6, 11, 16

HEER HALEWIJN (££)

A great place to sit by the fire in winter and taste some excellent wine with farmhouse cheeses or grills.

➕ blV ✉ Walplein 10 ☎ 33 92 61 🕐 Dinner only. Closed Mon & Tue 🚌 1

PAPILOTTE (££)

Small cosy restaurant in an old house with a garden. Very attentive service and French-inspired cuisine dictated by market supplies and prepared by the French chef and owner.

➕ clll ✉ Schaarstraat 70 ☎ 33 45 75 🕐 Wed–Sun dinner & Sun lunch. Closed Mon & Tue 🚌 1, 6

SIPHON (££)

Hugely popular restaurant outside Bruges serving Flemish specialities such as river eel in green herb sauce and grilled T-bone steaks. Very good value for money. Advance booking essential.

➕ Off map ✉ Damse Vaart Oost 1 ☎ 62 02 02 🕐 Lunch, dinner. Closed Thu, Fri 🚌 1.5km walk or taxi from Damme (▶ 21)

Belgian specialities

There is more to Belgian food than *moules frites*. *Waterzooi* is a little-known national dish, a stew of fish or chicken with leeks, parsley and cream. *Stoemp* is not unlike British bubble and squeak, often served with sausages. *Carbonnade flamande* is beef braised in beer with carrots and thyme and *lapin à la gueuze* is rabbit stewed in *gueuze* with prunes. River eels in green sauce, *anguilles au vert* is another popular dish.

INTERNATIONAL & EXOTIC CUISINE

Indonesian influences

Chinese food is rarely authentic in Belgian restaurants, often getting more inspiration from Indonesian cuisine. Almost every menu will have *loempia*, a big spring roll, or *nasi goreng*, Indonesian fried rice. And don't worry about the spices: you are unlikely to be putting your tastebuds at risk as most dishes are adapted to suit Belgian tastes.

BRUSSELS

AU THÉ DE PEKIN (£)
Authentic, refined Hong Kong cuisine and a few other Far Eastern specialities served in a simple room. Very good value.
E7 ☒ 16–24 rue de la Vierge Noire ☎ 513 4642 ☻ Lunch, dinner ⊜ Bourse/Beurs

LES BAGUETTES IMPERIALES (£££)
Belgium's only Michelin-starred oriental restaurant, serving refined and mouthwatering Vietnamese dishes.
D2–3 ☒ 70 avenue Jean Sobieski ☎ 479 6732 ☻ Lunch, dinner. Closed Sun dinner and Tue ☻ Stuyvenbergh ⊜ Bus 19, 23

LE BAR À TAPAS (£–££)
Well-prepared Spanish tapas are served with drinks, including a good selection of sherry. Comfortable chairs, low salon tables and often salsa music.
E7 ☒ 11, Rue Borgval Straat, off Place Saint-Géry/ Sint-Goriksplein ☎ 502 6602 ☻ Lunch, dinner. Closed Sat lunch, Sun ☻ Tram 23, 52, 55, 56, 81 (Bourse/Beurs)

CHEZ FATMA (£–££)
Fatma and Fergani Loussaifi are the king and queen of couscous. One of the best Tunisian restaurants in town.
G8 ☒ 18 place Jourdan ☎ 230 9597 ☻ Lunch, dinner. Closed Sat lunch and Sun ⊜ Bus 80

COMME CHEZ MOI (£)
Russian and Romanian cuisine in the heart of the Marolles district, best for caviar and blinis and a few shots of vodka or Russian wine.
E8 ☒ 140 rue Haute ☎ 502 5209 ☻ Lunch, dinner. Closed Mon ⊜ Bus 20, 48

COSI (££)
Smart, modern Italian restaurant popular with the Ixelles crowd. The simple décor is filled with furniture and objects from local junk markets. The food is good and light with excellent fresh pastas, good bruschetta and a delicious parma ham served with sweet pears.
F10 ☒ 95 rue Americaine/Amerikaansestraat ☎ 534 8586 ☻ Lunch and dinner. Closed Sat lunch, Sun ⊜ Tram 82; bus 54

DA KAO (£)
Cheap, popular eaterie serving good Vietnamese food to a trendy crowd on their way for a long night.
E7 ☒ 38 rue Antoine Dansaert ☎ 512 6716 ☻ Lunch, dinner ⊜ Bourse/Beurs ⊜ Tram 23, 52, 55, 56, 81

KASBAH, RESTAURANT & SALON (££)
A delightful dark blue Aladdin's cave, this trendy Moroccan restaurant surprises with a large menu of *tagines*, couscous and grills accompanied by longing, rhythmic Arabic music. The excellent Sunday brunch is very good value.
E7 ☒ 20 rue Antoine

Dansaertstraat ☎ 502 4026
🕐 Lunch, dinner. Closed Sat lunch 🚊 Tram 23, 52, 55, 56, 81 (Bourse/Beurs)

NEOS COSMOS (££)

Lively and trendy Greek eaterie serving excellent mezze in an attractive contemporary interior.
➕ E7 ✉ 50 rue Antoine Dansaert ☎ 511 8058
🕐 Lunch, dinner
🚇 Bourse/Beurs 🚊 Tram 23, 52, 55, 56, 81

NOCHE LATINA (£)

Cheap authentic South American dishes, like *ceviche* (raw marinated fish), accompanied by salsa music.
➕ E8 ✉ 204 rue Haute/Hoogstraat ☎ 502 0199
🕐 Lunch, dinner. Latin music in the evenings and disco at weekends 🚌 Bus 20, 48

LES PERLES DE PLUIE (££)

Wonderful Thai restaurant in a beautiful Brussels house.
➕ F9 ✉ 56 rue de Châtelaine ☎ 649 6723 🕐 Lunch, dinner. Closed Sat lunch and Mon
🚊 Tram 93, 94

BRUGES

BHAVANI (£–££)

Bruges' best Indian restaurant specialises in tandoori and vegetarian dishes like thalis and masala dosas, served in a pleasant bamboo décor.
➕ bIII ✉ Simon Stevinplein 5 ☎ 33 90 25 🕐 Lunch, dinner. Closed Tue 🚊 all

BODEGA LORENA (££)

Sr Rodrigues, the master of tapas, serves more than 60 tapas dishes, plenty of wines and beer. For a good time.
➕ bIII ✉ Loppemstraat 13 ☎ 34 88 17 🕐 Dinner. Closed Sun, Mon in winter 🚊 All

DE LANGE MUUR (£–££)

Chinese restaurant serving specialities from Canton, Fukien and Peking, renowned for its Chinese fondue and *rijsttafels*.
➕ bIII ✉ St Amandsplein 11 ☎ 33 27 19 🕐 Lunch, dinner
🚊 All

LE GRECO (££)

Good traditional Greek food prepared with fresh ingredients and served with a smile.
➕ bIII ✉ St Jacobsstraat 48 ☎ 33 02 96 🕐 Lunch, dinner. Closed Wed 🚊 3, 13

TANUKI (££)

Classic Japanese dishes served in an authentic interior with plenty of wood, a rock-tiled floor and a bamboo garden. Excellent sushi and tempura.
➕ bIV ✉ Oude Gentweg 1 ☎ 34 75 12 🕐 Lunch, dinner. Closed Mon & Tue 🚊 1, 11

TRIUM (£)

The best Italian restaurant in Bruges with fresh pasta and crunchy pizzas served by some of the most charming waiters outside Italy.
➕ bIII ✉ Academiestraat 23 ☎ 33 30 60 🕐 Tue–Thu 9–8, Fri–Sun 9–9. Closed Mon 🚊 4

Frites, frites, frites...

Belgium claims the best chips in the world. The secret of their *frites* is that they are fried twice and thrown in the air to get rid of the extra oil. Every Belgian has a favourite *friterie* or *frietkot*, but most will agree that Homage à Mafrite on the place du Jeu de Balle in Brussels is one of the best.

Bars & Cafés

Golden rule

Don't start visiting bars too early as many of the places don't fill up until after midnight.

A glass of beer

There are more than 400 varieties of Belgian beer and many of them come with their own glasses, specially designed to make the most of the beer's flavour and perfume. In the café La Lunette on the place de la Monnaie/Muntplein, an order for a 'lunette' means that the beer will be served in a 1-litre coupe (like an outsized champagne glass). In winter Belgians like to have their glass of beer accompanied by a tiny glass of *jenever*, a popular local spirit similar to gin. Guaranteed to warm you up!

BRUSSELS

Brussels can seem like a dull, grey city until you hit the bars. From elegant art-nouveau cafés and smoky old joints full of local pensioners to the crowded bars of rue du Marché au Charbon/Kolenmarkt, you'll find it all within walking distance of the Grand'Place.

A LA MORT SUBITE

This traditional bar was once one of the Belgian singer Jacques Brel's favourite watering holes and is still popular. It even has its own brew, the 'Mort Subite' or 'Sudden Death'.

✚ E7 ✉ 7 rue Montagne aux Herbes Potagères ☎ 512 8664 ⏰ Mon–Sat 11AM–1AM, Sun 12.30PM–1AM 🚇 Gare Centrale/Centraal station

L'ACROBATE

No point in getting to this kitsch bar with bright plastic roses early as most customers arrive after midnight. Dance floor at the back.

✚ E7 ✉ 14 rue Borgval ☎ 513 7308 ⏰ Fri, Sat 9–dawn 🚊 Tram 23, 52, 55, 56, 81, 90 (Bourse/Beurs)

AU SOLEIL

Popular bar in a former old-fashioned men's clothing shop with tables outside in summer.

✚ E7 ✉ 86 rue du Marché au Charbon ☎ 513 3430 ⏰ 10AM–2AM 🚊 Tram 23, 52, 55, 56, 81, 90 (Bourse/Beurs)

L'ESPÉRANCE

Wood-panelled art-deco bar, with a discreet staircase to rooms upstairs (said to be popular with politicians formerly), but now just a funky place to have a few drinks.

✚ E6 ✉ 1–3 rue du Finistère ☎ 217 3247 ⏰ Mon–Fri 10am–1am 🚇 De Brouckère

LE FALSTAFF

Huge but always busy art-deco café with a vast terrace (heated in winter) where everyone usually ends up at some time during an evening out, either for an aperitif or for an early morning coffee.

✚ E7 ✉ 19–25 rue Henri Maus ☎ 511 9877 ⏰ Mon–Fri 10.30AM–3AM; Sat–Sun 10.30AM–5AM 🚊 Tram 23, 52, 55, 56, 81, 90 (Bourse/Beurs)

H2 0

Romantic bar with candles, couples and classical music.

✚ E7 ✉ 27 rue du Marché au Charbon ☎ 512 3843 ⏰ 7PM–2AM 🚊 Tram 23, 52, 55, 56, 81, 90 (Bourse/Beurs)

KAFKA

Smoky brown bar with a wide selection of vodkas and Belgian beers, local eccentrics and dusty habitués. Pleasant, slightly bookish atmosphere mellows later at night when the vodka works on the rather serious Flemish intellectuals.

✚ E7 ✉ 6 rue de la Vierge Noire ☎ 513 5489 ⏰ Daily 4PM–3AM 🚇 De Brouckère

LE JAVA

Small, noisy bar, the perfect place to end a good evening out.

🔲 E7 ✉ 14 rue st Géry
☎ 512 3716 🕐 Mon–Sat
8PM–3AM; Sun noon–3AM
🚋 Tram 23, 52, 55, 56, 81, 90
(Bourse/Beurs)

LE SUD

Started as a squat several years ago, but even though Le Sud has gone legal it still swings. Good music and unreal Arabesque-Eurotrash building-site décor. Clo-Clo club in the cellar is a must if you have a longing for the seventies' French *chanson*. Worth a little search!

🔲 E7 ✉ 43 rue de l'Ecuyer/Schildknaapstraat (no sign, big sun mask above the entrance) ☎ No phone
🕐 Tue–Sun after 10PM 🚋 De Brouckère

DE ULTIEME HALLUCINATIE
(► 64–65)

ZEBRA

In a lively nightlife area and popular from breakfast onwards. Simple red-brick décor, outdoor terrace and good music.

🔲 E7 ✉ 35 place St-Géry/St Goriksplein ☎ 511 0901
🕐 7:30AM–1AM or later
🚋 Tram 23, 52, 55, 56, 81
(Bourse/Beurs)

BRUGES

DE CHAGALL

Cosy bar-restaurant with Belgian specialities, such as eel, ribsteaks and mussels, served to the accompaniment of classical music. Good choice for a coffee during the day or a liqueur after dinner..

🔲 bIII ✉ Sint-Amandstraat 40
☎ 33 61 12 🕐 Lunch, dinner
🚋 All

T'BRUGS BEERTJE

The place for the true beer lover, with a selection of over 300 traditionally brewed Belgian beers each served in its special glass (► panel opposite) The atmosphere is as Belgian as can be and the landlord will be happy to choose a beer to suit your personality. Many of these beers are rare and only on sale in this café.

🔲 bIII ✉ Kemelstraat 5
☎ 33 96 16 🕐 4PM–1AM.
Closed Wed 🚋 All

DE VLISSINGHE

Reputedly the oldest café in Bruges, built around 1515. The delightful 17th-century room has been used in films. Popular with locals as well as visitors.

🔲 dII ✉ Blekerstraat 2
☎ 34 37 37 🕐 Wed, Sat
2PM–1AM; Mon, Thu, Fri 4PM–1AM;
Sun 11:30AM–9PM. Closed Tue
🚋 4, 8

DE LOKKEDIZE

Popular candle-lit jazz café, often full, with the noisiest punters to be found around the bar. Light snacks are served.

🔲 bIII ✉ Korte Vulderstraat
33 ☎ 33 44 50 🕐 Tue–Thu
7PM–3AM, Fri–Sun 6PM–3AM or
later. Closed Mon 🚋 4, 8

Beer in Bruges

There are still two breweries in the town centre. De Gouden Boom in de Langestraat makes Tarwebier, a wheat beer recommended with a slice of lemon, and a stronger brew called Brugse Tripel with a 9.5 per cent alcohol content. De Straffe Hendrik (✉ Walplein 26 ☎ 33 26 97) brews another wheat beer with a sweet aroma.

LACE

Chinese lace

Belgium has long been famous for the finest lace in the world but today few Belgian women learn the craft. As a result, there is not enough hand-made lace to meet the demand and what there is has become very expensive. Many shops now sell lace made in China, which is cheaper but often of an inferior quality.

BRUSSELS

LACE GALLERY

Tiny old-fashioned shop selling good-quality hand-made lace blouses, tablecloths, umbrellas, cushion covers etc.

✚ E7 ✉ 30 rue du Lombard, corner rue de l'Etuve ☎ 513 5830 🕐 10–7 🚊 Tram 23, 52, 55, 56, 81, 90 (Bourse/Beurs)

LACE PALACE

Spacious lace shop selling everything that can possibly be made of lace, both Belgian and imported, old and new.

✚ E7 ✉ 1–3 rue de la Violette ☎ 512 5634 🕐 Daily 8:30–8 🚇 Gare Centrale

RUBBRECHT

Elegant shop with an exquisite collection of old lace pieces, table cloths and blouses as well as new Belgian hand-made lace. Definitely a cut above the rest, with no imported stock.

✚ E7 ✉ 23 Grand'Place ☎ 512 0218 🕐 Mon–Sat 9:30–7; Sun 10–6 🚇 Gare Centrale/Centraal Station

TOEBAC

One of the better lace shops in a street lined with them. A wide selection of blouses, tablecloths and modern and antique lace, mostly made in Belgium.

✚ E7 ✉ 10 rue Charles Buls ☎ 512 0941 🕐 9:30–7 🚊 Tram 23, 52, 55, 56, 81, 90 (Bourse/Beurs)

BRUGES

'TAPOSTELIENTJE

Tiny, pretty shop selling hand-made lace, both modern and antique, as well as everything to make lace. Professional advice on everything you always wanted to know about lace.

✚ clll ✉ Balstraat 11 ☎ 33 78 60 🕐 Mon–Sat 9:30–6; Sun 11–4 🚌 6, 16

GRUUTHUSE LACE SHOP

The place to look for good quality lace, especially antique pieces. All lace is certified 'made in Belgium'. Another speciality is handmade porcelain dolls dressed in antique lace.

✚ blll ✉ Dijver 15 ☎ 34 30 54 🕐 Summer 10–7; Winter 10–6:30 🚌 1, 6, 11, 16

KANTCENTRUM (LACE CENTRE)

Historical and technical exhibits. Demonstrations of lace-making in the afternoons and materials for lace-making on sale. Interesting courses.

✚ clll ✉ Peperstraat 3A ☎ 33 00 72 🕐 Mon–Fri 10–12 & 2–6; Sat 10–12 & 2–5. Closed Sun 💷 Cheap

KANTJUWEELTJE (LACE JEWEL)

Wide selection of new and antique hand-made Flemish lace as well as tapestries. Lace-making demonstrations 3 pm daily.

✚ blll ✉ Philipstockstraat 11 ☎ 33 42 25 🕐 Summer 9–7, winter 9–6 🚌 4, 8

CRAFTS, SOUVENIRS & GIFTS

BRUSSELS

AU GRAND RASOIR (MAISON JAMART)

A beautiful specialist knife shop, supplier to the Royal family, which also repairs, sharpens and re-silvers knives. An incredible selection for every possible purpose.

✚ E7 ✉ 7 rue de l'Hôpital (place St Jean) ☎ 512 4962 ⏲ Mon–Sat 9:30–6:30 🚇 Gare Centrale/Centraal Station 🚌 Bus 34, 48, 95, 96

THE BRUSSELS CORNER

Better-quality and more fun souvenirs than in most shops, with a large collection of T-shirts and gift boxes with Belgian beers.

✚ E7 ✉ 27 rue de l'Etuve/Stoofstraat ☎ 511 9849 ⏲ 9:30–6:30 🚌 Bus 34, 48

LA BOUTIQUE DE TINTIN

The destination for Tintin fans with everything from pyjamas, socks, cups and diaries to life-size statues of Tintin and his friend Abdullah, made to order, and, of course, the books in several languages..

✚ E7 ✉ 13 rue de la Colline ☎ 514 5152 ⏲ Tue–Thu 10–6, Mon 2–6 🚇 Gare Centrale/Centraal Station

CHRISTA RENIERS

Beautiful contemporary jewellery with a touch of Zen, but never short of humour. Her silver cufflinks and keyrings are fun and her bracelets, rings and earrings have an elegance all of their own.

✚ E7 ✉ 28 rue du Vieux Marché aux Grains/Oude Graanmarkt ☎ 514 1773 ⏲ Thu–Sat 12–7 🚋 Tram 23, 52, 55, 56, 81; bus 63

KASOERI

A great fabric shop selling linen in natural colours, silks and wools, brightly coloured Indian cottons and buttons made of coral or mother-of-pearl.

✚ F8 ✉ 20 rue de la Paix/Vredestraat ☎ 514 2251 ⏲ Mon–Sat 10:30–6:30 🚇 Porte de Namur/Naamse Poort

BRUGES

BRUGS DIAMANTHUIS

The technique of diamond-polishing is attributed to the Bruges goldsmith van Berquem (mid-15th century) and Bruges was Europe's first diamond city. This shop revives the tradition with a large selection of quality diamonds and diamond jewellery.

✚ dll ✉ Cordoeanierstraat 5 ☎ 34 41 60 ⏲ Mon–Fri 10–12, 1:30–5; Sat 10–3 🚌 6, 16

KERAMIEK ANNE PERNEEL

Unusual, earthy ceramics for everyday use and ornate flowerpots for the garden. It is wonderful to see this inventive potter at work and somehow her enthusiasm is contagious.

✚ dll ✉ Genthof 29 ☎ 82 38 38 ⏲ Sat 10–12, 1:30–6 🚌 4, 8

Original birthday presents

Dans la presse ce–jour–là (In the press that day) ✉ 126 rue Antoine Dansaertstraat ☎ 511 4389 sells original copies of newspapers in several languages, printed on the recipient's day of birth. Or how about a life-size Manneken Pis fountain for the garden? – available from shops around Manneken Pis (► 27) on the rue de l'Etuve/Stoofstraat.

BOOKS

Expensive business

The mark-up on foreign books is often high, so it is cheaper to buy books at home or try second-hand stores. Galerie Bortier in Brussels has a good selection. The Deslegte chain sells second-hand books and discounted new books at 17 rue des Grandes Carmes in Brussels (☎ 511 6140) or at Vlamingstraat 37–9 in Bruges (☎ 34 04 39).

BRUSSELS

BRÜSEL
Large bookshop selling famous comic strips such as Tintin and Asterix, mainly in French but also in Dutch, English, German and Spanish.
✚ E7 ✉ 100 boulevard Anspach ☎ 502 3552 🕐 Mon–Sat 10:30–6:30 🚋 Tram 23, 52, 55, 56, 81

FNAC
Brussels' largest bookshop with books in French and Dutch as well as a good selection of English, German, Italian and Spanish and an excellent music department.
✚ F6 ✉ City2, rue Neuve/Nieuwstraat ☎ 209 2211 🕐 Mon–Thu, Sat 10–7; Fri 10–8 🚇 Rogier or De Brouckère 🚋 Tram 23, 52, 55, 56, 81

P GENICOT
A lovely bookshop selling books from the 17th century until now, mainly French, but some in English.
✚ E7 ✉ 6 galerie Bortier on 19 rue St Jean/St Jansstraat ☎ 514 1017 🕐 Mon–Sat 12–7 🚇 Gare Centrale/Centraal Station

IMAGE
Books in several languages on Belgian monuments, architecture and monument conservation packed into a small shop.
✚ E7 ✉ 72 rue de la Montagne/Bergstraat ☎ 512 2272 🕐 Mon–Fri 11–5 🚇 Gare Centrale/Centraal Station

W H SMITH
Part of the British chain, with a good selection of English books and magazines, and an ordering service.
✚ E6 ✉ 71–5 blvd Adolphe Max ☎ 219 2708 🕐 Mon, Wed–Sat 9–6:30; Tue 10–6:30 🚇 Rogier 🚋 Tram 23, 52, 55, 56, 81

TROPISMES
Very open and stylish bookshop in elegant gallery with a wide selection of books on art, architecture, history, philosophy etc. Specialises in good-quality coffee-table books and French literature, but also a wide selection of English-language books. A pleasant place to browse.
✚ E7 ✉ galerie des Princes ☎ 512 8852 🕐 Mon, Sun 1:30–6:30, Tue–Thu, Sat 10–6:30, Fri 10:30–8 🚇 Gare Centrale/Centraal Station

BRUGES

DE REYGHERE
Books in Flemish, French, English and German and a wide selection of international newspapers and magazines.
✚ bIII ✉ Markt 12 ☎ 33 34 03 🕐 Mon–Thu, Sat 8:30–6:15, Fri 8:30–7. Closed Sun 🚌 All buses

RAAKLIJN
Bruges' best bookshop with a good selection of foreign-language books, especially paperbacks and art books.
✚ bIII ✉ St Jacobsstraat 7 ☎ 33 67 20 🕐 Mon–Sat 9–6:30 🚌 All buses

ANTIQUES &
BROCANTE (SECOND-HAND)

BRUSSELS

AMAZONITE
Aladdin's little treasure cave filled to the brim with North African antiques and bric-à-brac. Nothing too valuable, but interesting and fun.

E8 ☒ 11 rue Blaesstraat ☎ 075 622 711 ⏰ 10–6 🚌 Bus 20, 21, 48

ANTIK BLAES
Two floors of old and funky European furniture, fifties-style office shelves, old shop furniture and a few strange *objets*.

E8 ☒ 51–3 rue Blaesstraat ☎ 512 1299 ⏰ 10–6 🚌 Bus 20, 21, 48

GALERIE MODERNE
Huge auction house selling the full range from top-of-the-market antiques to junk and bric-à-brac.

F–G8 ☒ 3 rue du Parnasse ☎ 511 5415 ⏰ Twice a month. Phone for viewing times 🚇 Trône/Troon 🚌 Bus 38, 54, 60, 95, 96

GALERIE VANDERKINDERE
Upmarket auction house specialising in art and objects from the 17th and 18th centuries.

D–E11 ☒ 512 rue em Vanderkindere ☎ 344 5446 ⏰ Mon–Fri 9–12, 2–5. Phone for times of sale 🚌 Tram 23, 55; bus 38

GHADIMI
Fine collection of mainly 19th-century oriental carpets, kilims and textiles stylishly presented in this bright gallery.

E8 ☒ 1 rue des Minimes, just off the place du Grand Sablon ☎ 512 9841 ⏰ Tue–Sun 10–12, 2–6. Closed Mon 🚌 Tram 92, 93, 94; bus 34, 48, 95, 96

HISTORIC MARINE
Old and antique boat and ship models as well as antique compasses, marine instruments and paintings of boats.

E7 ☒ 39a rue du Lombardstraat ☎ 513 8155 ⏰ Mon–Sat 9:30–5:30 🚌 Bus 34, 49, 95, 96

PUCCI
A fascinating shop full of art-deco and art-nouveau chandeliers, furniture and *objets d'art*.

E8 ☒ 13 rue de la Paille ☎ 512 7889 ⏰ Mon–Sat 10–5:30 🚌 Bus 34, 48, 95, 96

STYLE & KEZOEN
Wide selection of old fountain pens from famous manufacturers are bought, sold and repaired here.

E8 ☒ 124 rue Blaesstraat ☎ 387 0122 ⏰ Tue, Thu–Sat 9–2 🚌 Bus 20, 48

BRUGES

G P TRAEN
Big and interesting antique shop with some very ornate or rather unusual European furniture, sculpture and porcelain.

bIII ☒ St Amandsstraat 37 ☎ 33 49 24 ⏰ Mon–Sat 9–12, 2–6 🚌 All buses

Antiques in Brussels
Go to Brussels' Sablon area (➤ 30) for upmarket antiques, and the junk market in the Marolles (➤ 26, 58) if you want to browse or bargain hunt. Junk and antique shops on rue Haute/Hoogstraat and the rue Blaesstraat are good for furniture but becoming fashionable. Check out the streets behind the church on place du Jeu de Balles.

FOOD

Belgian beers

Lambic is a beer which ferments spontaneously. *Gueuze* is a mixture of *lambics*, while sweet *kriek* is *lambic* with cherries. Trappist beers come as *doubels* with 6–7 per cent alcohol or *tripels* at 8 or 9 per cent. A lighter, refreshing beer is the *bierre blanche* or *witbier*, made of wheat and often drunk with a slice of lemon.

BRUSSELS

AU SUISSE
The best place for sandwiches and a Brussels institution, with an incredible selection of breads and spreads, salads, smoked fish, cheeses and *charcuterie* or cold cuts. Try their speciality, *filet Américain*, a steak tartare, perfect for getting you back on course after a night on the town.
➕ E7 ✉ 73–5 boulevard Anspach ☎ 512 9589
🕐 Mon–Sat 8:30–7 🚊 Tram 23, 52, 55, 56, 81 (Bourse/Beurs)

BIÈRE ARTISANALE
Over 400 Belgian beers and their appropriate glasses. The gift packages are a good idea for presents.
➕ F8 ✉ 174 Chausée de Wavre ☎ 512 1788
🕐 Mon–Sat 11–7 🚇 Porte de Namur/Naamse Poort

DANDOY
A beautiful bakery shop, founded in 1829, selling traditional Brussels biscuits such as Pain à la Grecque, Speculoos and Coucque de Dinant in all sizes and shapes as well as Belgium's best marzipan. Once you are in it is hard to resist!
➕ E7 ✉ 31 rue au Beurre/Boterstraat (new branch 14 rue Charles Buls) ☎ 511 0326 🕐 Mon–Sat 8:30–6:30, Sun 10–6:30 🚊 Tram 23, 52, 55, 56, 81 (Bourse/Beurs)

LE PAIN QUOTIDIEN/HET DAGELIJKS BROOD
(► 64)

WITTAMER
Wonderful but seriously expensive patisserie with the best sorbets in town, excellent hand-made chocolates and gâteaux that taste as good as they look. *Dégustations* on the terrace.
➕ E8 ✉ 12–13 place du Grand Sablon/Grote Zavel ☎ 512 3742 🕐 Mon 8–6, Tue–Sat 7–7, Sun 7–6 🚊 Tram 92, 93, 94; bus 34, 48, 95, 96

BRUGES

DELDYCKE
Wide selection of Belgian and other cheeses, *charcuterie* and prepared salads, as well as wine and liqueurs.
➕ bIII ✉ Wollestraat 23 ☎ 33 43 35 🕐 9–2, 3–6:30. Closed Tue 🚌 1, 6, 11, 16

TEMMERMAN
Good-quality old-fashioned sweets, sugared almonds, *speculoos*, fine hand-made chocolates in the shape of seafood or pebbles, all stored in great jars. Also try the heart-shaped *peperkoek*, a spicy honey bread, or their large selection of fruity teas.
➕ bIII ✉ Zilverpand, Noordzandstraat 63 ☎ 33 16 78 🕐 Mon 2–6:30, Tue–Thu 10–12:30, 2–6:30, Fri, Sat 10–6:30. Closed Sun, Mon am 🚌 All buses

WOOLSTREET COMPANY
Small shop selling more than 450 Belgian beers and their special glasses.
➕ bIII ✉ Wollestraat 31a ☎ 34 83 83 🕐 10–7 🚌 1, 6, 11, 16

CHOCOLATES

The Swiss claim that they produce the best chocolate in the world is hotly disputed in Belgium. The Swiss may market it more effectively, but Belgian chocolate is as good if not better.

BRUSSELS

GALLER

Belgian Royal Warrant Holder, so if it is good enough for the King of the Belgians it must be all right! Very good pralines and delicious chocolate bars in many flavours.

✚ E7 ✉ 44 rue au Beurre/Boterstraat ☎ 502 0266 🕐 Daily 10–9:30 🚋 Tram 23, 52, 55, 56, 81 (Bourse/Beurs)

GODIVA

The most famous of all, with shops around the world. A feast for the eyes and the mouth.

✚ E7 ✉ 22 Grand'Place ☎ 511 2537 🕐 Mon–Sat 9am–midnight, Sun 10am–midnight 🚇 Gare Centrale/Centraal Station

NEUHAUS

The most beautiful of the many Neuhaus branches. Divine chocolates in astonishing gift boxes. Try specialities like Caprice (chocolate with nougatine and fresh cream) or Temptatio (coffee and fresh cream).

✚ E7 ✉ 25–7 Galerie de la Reine/Koninginnegallerij ☎ 512 6359 🕐 Mon–Sat 9–8, Sun 10–7 🚇 Gare Centrale/Centraal Station 🚋 Tram 23, 52, 55, 56, 81 (Bourse/Beurs)

PLANÈTE CHOCOLAT

'Chocolate is art' is Frank Duval's slogan. You can watch him make and sculpt wonderful artworks or pralines on the premises from the best chocolate. Serious chocoholics will want to eat them there and then, but on the first floor is a tea room with chocolates, cakes and ice creams.

✚ E7 ✉ 57 rue du Midi ☎ 511 0755 🕐 Daily 9–6:30, on beautiful days until 10pm 🚋 Tram 23, 52, 55, 56, 81 (Bourse/Beurs)

WITTAMER ➤ 74

BRUGES

DEPLA

Delicious hand-made chocolates. Specialities include truffles, florentines, chocolates with nuts and raisins and good marzipan wrapped in chocolate. Recommended.

✚ bIII ✉ Huidenvettersplein 13 ☎ 34 74 12 🕐 Daily 10–6:30 🚌 6, 16. Also at Eekhoutstraat 23 (☎ 33 49 53)

GODIVA

The Bruges branch of this superlative chocolatier.

✚ bIII ✉ Zuidzandstraat 36 ☎ 33 28 66 🕐 Mon–Sat 9–12:30, 2–7. Closed Sun 🚌 All buses

SWEERTVAEGHER

Superior and luxurious hand-made pralines, much appreciated locally.

✚ bIII ✉ Philipstockstraat 29 ☎ 33 83 67 🕐 Tue–Sat 9:30–6:30 🚌 6, 16

Chocolate chains

The Leonidas chain, cheaper than the shops mentioned here, sells very good quality chocolates, and the beautifully wrapped Côte d'Or bars are worth seeking out in supermarkets.

BELGIAN FASHION

Brussels shopping streets

Avenue Louise (➤ 35) is the traditional shopping area with everything from Chanel to the Belgian designer Olivier Strelli, but recently rue Antoine Dansaert has become the Mecca for Belgian fashion. Apart from the several Stijl shops, other shops and new designers have opened their doors including Michel Demulder. Well worth checking out if you are into the latest trends!

BRUSSELS

ELVIS POMPILLO
Some very wearable and some outrageous hats for men, women and kids, always with a quirky twist, by a Liège-born hatmaker who really *is* called Elvis Pompillo.
➕ E7 ✉ 10 rue du Midi/Zuidstraat ☎ 511 1188 🕐 Mon–Sat 10:30–6:30 🚊 Tram 23, 52, 55, 56, 81; bus 34, 48

KAAT TILLEY
Tilley's loose, sculptured clothes for women in amazing fabrics defy description, while the shop belongs in a fairy tale rather than in this elegant gallery. Her clothes are hugely popular in Japan and in New York, where she has opened two more shops.
➕ E7 ✉ Galerie du Roi 4 ☎ 514 0763 🕐 Mon–Fri 10–6, Sat 10:30–6:30 🚉 Gare Centrale/Centraal Station 🚊 Bus 29, 63, 66, 71

MICHEL DEMULDER (THE STOCK)
This young designer is quickly making a name for himself, especially amongst young media stars. The shop also sells end-of-range stock from other designers.
➕ E6 ✉ 11/13 rue Lepage ☎ 512 5533 🕐 11–6:30. Closed Sun, Mon am and Tue 🚊 Tram 23, 52, 55, 56, 81(Bourse/Beurs); bus 63

OLIVIER STRELLI
Streamlined modern fashion for men and women in blacks, beiges, greys and browns, and an occasional dash of colour. Both classic and very contemporary.
➕ F9 ✉ 72 avenue Louise ☎ 512 5607 🕐 Mon–Sat 10–6 🚊 Tram 93, 94

STIJL
Grand temple of Belgian fashion, selling the collections of established designers such as Dries van Noten, Bikkembergs – as well as the newcomers, in bare and cold industrial surroundings. The Stijl sells men's and women's clothes, while on the same street there are sister shops selling trendy kiddies clothes (Kat en Muis) and beautiful lingerie (Stijl Underwear, No 47).
➕ E7 ✉ 74 rue Antoine Dansaert ☎ 512 0313 🕐 Mon–Sat 10:30–6:30 🚊 Tram 23, 52, 55, 56, 81; bus 63

BRUGES

L'HEROÏNE
The only shop in Bruges with a wide selection of Belgian fashion designers, including Kaat Tilley, Chris Janssens and Dries Van Noten. Also fashion accessories and Belgian jewellery.
➕ bIII ✉ Zilverpand 5, Noordzandstraat 57b ☎ 33 56 57 🕐 Mon–Sat 10–6:30 🚊 All buses

Offbeat & Unusual

BRUSSELS

AZZATO

Musical instruments, especially string instruments and flutes but with a large selection of ethnic instruments especially drums.

🔒 E7 ✉ 42 rue de la Violette/Violetstraat ☎ 512 37 52 🚊 Tram 23, 52, 55, 56, 81 (Bourse/Beurs)

CONDOMI

The place for condoms, from the straightforward to the exotic, also for people with allergies or special needs.

🔒 E7 ✉ 37 rue des Pierres/Steenstraat ☎ 513 5983 ☎ Mon–Sat 12–6 🚊 Tram 23, 52, 55, 56, 81

LA COURTE ECHELLE

Exquisite dolls' houses and everything to go inside them. Upstairs, classes to help you make your own miniatures.

🔒 E7 ✉ 12 rue des Eperonniers ☎ 512 4759 ☎ Mon–Tue, Thu–Sat 11–1:30, 2–6 🚊 Gare Centrale/Centraal Station

PICARD

Europe's largest party house is a wonderful place. Fancy dresses for sale or rent, masks, party tricks and magicians' equipment.

🔒 E7 ✉ 71–5 rue du Lombardstraat ☎ 513 0790 ☎ Mon–Sat 9–6 🚌 Bus 34, 48

ROYAL DOG SHOP

'Le Couturier pour Chiens' says it all. Diamond collars, cardigans, raincoats and accessories for the comfort and elegance of your dog or cat. Made to measure or ready-made.

🔒 E7 ✉ 27–28 place de la Justice/Justitieplein ☎ 513 3261 ☎ Mon, Wed–Sat 9–6. Closed Tue 🚌 Bus 34, 48

SERNEELS

A spacious shop with a wonderful selection of good-quality toys that will revive memories of your own childhood. Cuddly toys from tiny ducklings to full-size camels, cars, old-fashioned rocking horses etc.

🔒 F9 ✉ 69 avenue Louise ☎ 538 3066 ☎ Mon–Sat 9:30–6:30 🚊 Tram 93, 94

LA VAISELLE AU KILO

China, glass and cutlery, mostly sold by the kilo.

🔒 E8 ✉ 8a rue Bodenbroeckstraat, off the place du Grand Sablon/Grote Zavel ☎ 513 49 84 ☎ Mon–Sat 10–6, Sun 10–5:30 🚌 Bus 48

BRUGES

OUD TEGELHUIS

Amusing shop, in two old houses, stocking all kinds of bygone tins and posters.

🔒 clII ✉ Peerdenstraat 11 ☎ 34 01 03 ☎ Tue–Sun 10–6 Closed Mon 🚌 1, 6, 11, 16

ROMBAUX

Lovely old-fashioned music store with CDs, instruments, sheet music. Worth a detour for the décor!

🔒 clII ✉ Mallebergstraat 13 ☎ 33 25 75 ☎ Mon–Sat 9–12:30, 2–6:30. Closed Sun 🚌 All buses to the Markt

Old-fashioned toys

'In den Olifant' is a chain of toy shops selling beautifully made wooden toys, mobiles, puppets and a large selection of creative toys and musical instruments. In Brussels at ✉ 47 rue des Fripiers/Kleerkopersstraat ☎ 217 4397. In Bruges at ✉ St Jacobsstraat 47 ☎ 32 75 79. Pricey but worth every franc.

JAZZ, POP & NIGHTLIFE

Clubbing

Most clubs open at 11 PM but don't start to fill before midnight. Belgians go out often because there are so many good bars. Englishmen or Australians, used to drinking up before the pubs close at 11 PM, may need some stamina. It's customary to buy rounds for your friends or whoever paid the last one.

BRUSSELS

L'ACROBATE (► 68)

ANCIENNE BELGIQUE
One of Brussels' best rock venues revamped as the showcase for the Flemish community and a counterpart to the Botanique. Regular concerts by major artists. Smaller club on the first floor for gigs.
✚ E7 ✉ 114 boulevard Anspachlaan ☎ 584 2400 🚋 Tram 23, 52, 55, 56, 81

BEURSSCHOUWBURG
The 19th-century theatre of the Stock Exchange is now a venue for rock concerts, good jazz, North African rai and Belgian avant-garde theatre.
✚ E7 ✉ 22 rue Auguste Ortsstraat ☎ 513 8290 🚋 Tram 23, 52, 55, 56, 81; bus 34, 47, 48, 63, 95, 96

BOTANIQUE/ BOTANIEK
The splendid botanical gardens were turned into a cultural centre for Brussels' French-speaking community. Regular rock concerts in the Orangerie and, increasingly, world music events. Festival de la Chanson in- and outdoors during September.
✚ F6 ✉ 236 rue Royale/ Koningsstraat ☎ 226 1211 Ⓜ Botanique 🚋 Tram 92, 94; bus 38, 61

CARNOA QUEBRADA
One of several Latin American clubs in this area. Strong *caipirinhas* make dancing to salsa music much easier.
✚ E7 ✉ 53 rue du Marché au Charbon/Kolenmarkt ☎ 511 1354 🕐 Tue 9:30–early morning, Wed–Sun 10:30–dawn 🚋 Tram 23, 52, 55, 56, 81

CIRQUE ROYAL/ KONINKLIJK CIRKUS
Great circular hall in a former circus, with usherettes to show you to your seat. Good gigs.
✚ F7 ✉ 81 rue de l'Enseignement/Onderwijsstraat ☎ 218 2015 Ⓜ Madou 🚌 Bus 29, 63

EXITO 13
South American club with good value Latino food, tasty jazz and the best Brazilian salsa groups.
✚ E8 ✉ 13 rue Haute/Hoogstraat ☎ 511 0038 🕐 Tue–Sat 7PM until the punters go home 🚌 Bus 20, 48

FOREST NATIONAL/VORST NATIONAAL
One of Belgium's largest venues, unfortunately with a reputation for bad acoustics and endless parking problems. Still, many major bands and stars insist on performing here when in the country.
✚ C11 ✉ avenue du Globelaan ☎ 347 0355 🕐 All year round 🚋 Tram 18, 52; bus 48, 54

THE FUSE
Brussels' first techno club maintains excellent standards with DJs from London, the States and Amsterdam. Located in a former Spanish disco, the décor is drab but the crowds don't seem to notice.
✚ E8 ✉ 208 rue Blaesstraat

☎ 511 9789 ⏰ Sat 11PM–7AM
🚌 Bus 20, 48 Ⓜ Porte de Hal

KK (KULTUURKAFEE)

Smoky student club at the Flemish University VUB, with free weekly gigs of small local and European bands, good art films and interesting exhibitions in the first-floor gallery. Lively atmosphere.
✚ H–J10 ✉ VUB campus boulevard du Triomphe ☎ 629 3056 ⏰ Concerts Oct–end Apr 🚊 Tram 23, 90; bus 34

MAGASIN 4

This former warehouse is a smaller venue, where many upcoming rock bands have performed for the first time in the country. It's a great place to watch new Flemish bands as well.
✚ E6 ✉ 4 rue du Magasin ☎ 223 3474 ⏰ Check listings Ⓜ Yser 🚊 Tram 18

MIRANO CONTINENTAL

Trendy crowds frequent this former cinema where house music is king.
✚ G7 ✉ 38 chaussée de Louvain/Leuvensesteenweg ☎ 218 5772 ⏰ Sat 11PM–late Ⓜ Madou 🚌 Bus 29, 63

SOUNDS

Cosy bar run by Italians with a small stage at the back for local and touring jazz musicians.
✚ F8 ✉ 28 rue de la Tulipe/Tulpstraat ☎ 512 9250 ⏰ Mon–Fri 11:30AM–late, Sat 7PM–late Ⓜ Porte de Namur/Naamse Poort 🚌 Bus 34, 54, 71, 80

LE SUD (▶ 69)

UPSIDE DOWN

Bar with paintings of tribesmen on the walls, a dance floor at the back and DJs playing excellent African music, soul and funk. Occasional live music.
✚ E7 ✉ 24 rue du Lombardstraat ☎ 511 0093 ⏰ Daily 7PM–4AM 🚊 Tram 23, 52, 55, 56, 81, 90; bus 34, 48, 95, 96

BRUGES

DE CACTUS CLUB

The main venue in town for rock, jazz and world music concerts. They also organise an open-air festival in the Minnewater Park during the second weekend of July. Their music café recently opened at No 36 on the same street.
✚ bIII ✉ St Jacobsstraat 33 ☎ 33 20 14 🚌 3, 13

DE VERSTEENDE NACHT

Cosy, smoky café run by a jazz afficionado. Often free jazz concerts at weekends.
✚ dIII ✉ Langestraat 11 ☎ 34 32 93 ⏰ Tue–Thu 7PM–2AM, Fri 7PM–4AM. Closed Sun, Mon

VILLA ROMANA

Popular discothèque, especially crowded at weekends.
✚ bIII ✉ Kraanplein 1 ☎ 34 34 53 ⏰ Daily 10PM–late 🚌 3, 4, 6, 8, 13, 16

Gay Brussels

The two lesbian bars are Le Feminin (✉ 9 rue Borgval ⏰ Tue, Thu–Sat 10PM–late) and Sapho (✉ 1 rue St Géry ⏰ Fri, Sat 10PM–late). There are bars for gay men around rue des Pierres as well as Le Belgica (✉ 32 rue du Marché au Charbon), Le Duquesnoy (✉ 12 rue Duquesnoy), with barmen in leather, and La Démence (✉ 208 rue Blaes).

OPERA & CLASSICAL MUSIC

Music by the coal stove

L'Atelier (✉ 51 rue du Commerce ☎ 511 2065 🚇 Trône/Troon), the former workshop of a painter and his wife who were both music lovers, is filled with canvases and memorabilia and is now a popular place for concerts. Many famous musicians have performed here. In winter it is heated by a big coal stove in the middle of the room.

BRUSSELS

CHAPELLE ROYALE
Beautiful small hall with perfect acoustics, a favourite with chamber orchestras. Book early as there are only 150 seats.
➕ F7–8 ✉ 5 Coudenberg ☎ 673 0581 🚇 Gare Centrale/Centraal Station

CONSERVATOIRE ROYALE DE MUSIQUE
Another perfect venue for chamber orchestras and voice recitals, partly designed by the famous organ builder Cavaillé-Coll. Preliminary selections for the Concours International Reine Elisabeth are held here.
➕ F7 ✉ 30 rue de la Régence/Regentschapstraat ☎ Box office 507 8200 in the Palais de Beaux Arts 🚇 Gare Centrale/Centraal Station

EGLISE DES ST JEAN ET ST ETIENNE AUX MINIMES
Many concerts are held in this high-baroque church near the Marolles quarter. The Philharmonic Society has early-music recitals and on Sundays the La Chapelle des Minimes ensemble performs Bach cantatas. Admission fees are voluntary.
➕ E8 ✉ 62 rue des Minimes ☎ 511 9384 🕐 Lunch time throughout the summer. One Sun a month at 10:30am 🚌 Bus 48

PALAIS DES BEAUX ARTS/PALEIS VOOR SCHONE KUNSTEN
This art-nouveau complex is Brussels' most prestigious concert venue. Its two halls with perfect acoustics are home to the Philharmonic Society and the Orchestre National de Belgique. Organises most of the big concerts in the city.
➕ F7 ✉ 23 rue Ravensteinstraat ☎ Box office 507 8200, 24-hour info 507 8444 🕐 Box office Mon–Sat 11–6 🚇 Parc/Park

THÉÂTRE DE LA MONNAIE/ MUNTSCHOUWBURG
The national opera house is Brussels' pride. After a sumptuous renovation in the 1980s, the then director Gerard Mortier boldly steered it towards innovative first-class performances. The current director Bernard Foccroulle, himself a musician, continues the success story. Performances are usually sold out well in advance. (► 55)
➕ E7 ✉ place de la Monnaie/Muntplein ☎ 229 1211 🕐 Box office Tue–Sat 11–5:30 🚇 De Brouckère

BRUGES

CULTUURCENTRUM
Four venues under one name, including the Stadsschouwburg, the city's theatre, with performances mostly in Flemish, and good classical concerts.
➕ bIII ✉ St Jacobsstraat 20–26 ☎ Information 44 30 40 box office 44 30 60 🕐 Box office Mon–Fri 10–1 & 2–6, Sat 10–1 🚇 All buses

80

THEATRE & DANCE

BRUSSELS

CIRQUE ROYAL/ KONINKLIJK CIRKUS (► 78)
Best dance theatre, mostly for contemporary dance.

KAAITHEATER
Influential, mainly Belgian, artists such as Anne Teresa de Keersmaeker, Jan Fabre and Maatschappij Discordia regularly perform here.

➕ E5–6 ✉ 2 quai des Péniches/Akenkaai ☎ Info: 2015858; box office 201 5959 Ⓜ Yser

LUNATHEATER
A jewel of thirties architecture, this former cinema houses the Flemish Theatre Institute .

➕ D6 ✉ 20 place Sainctelettesquare ☎ Box office 201 5959 Ⓜ Yser

THÉÂTRE 140
Rather scruffy theatre but excellent performances, both dance and theatre, by the best tour groups.

➕ H6 ✉ 140 avenue Eugène Plaskylaan ☎ 733 9708 🕐 Box office Mon–Sat 11–6 🚋 Tram 23, 90; bus 29, 63

THEATRE DE LA BALSAMINE
Very experimental dance and theatre venue in a eerie former barracks.

➕ H6 ✉ 1 avenue Felix Marchal ☎ 735 6468 🕐 Box Office Mon–Fri 10–6 🚌 Bus 29, 54

THÉÂTRE NATIONAL
The National Theatre often arranges co-productions with Strasbourg. Most plays are in French, with the occasional English-speaking/British touring company.

➕ F6 ✉ Centre Rogier, place Rogierplein ☎ 203 5303 🕐 Box office Mon–Sat 11–6 Ⓜ Rogier

THÉÂTRE ROYAL DU PARC
Stunning theatre with excellent French productions as well as old-fashioned and now unique 1930s *pièces de boulevard*.

➕ F7 ✉ 3 rue de la Loi/Wetstraat ☎ 512 2339 🕐 Daily 11–6 Ⓜ Arts–Loi/ Kunst/Wet or Parc

THÉÂTRE DE TOONE
Adorable little marionette theatre, famous for productions of theatre classics such as Hamlet and Faust performed in Bruxellois, the Brussels dialect which is a wierd mixture of French and Flemish. The fun café is open all day.

➕ E7 ✉ 6 impasse Schuddeveld, petite rue des Bouchers ☎ 511 7137 🕐 Tue–Sat noon–midnight Ⓜ Gare Centrale/Centraal Station

BRUGES

CULTUURCENTRUM
Four venues under one name ► 80.

➕ blll ✉ St Jacobsstraat 20–26 ☎ Info 44 30 40, box office 44 30 60 🕐 Box office Mon–Fri 10–1 & 2–6, Sat 10–1 Ⓜ All buses

Belgium dances

Belgium's reputation for contemporary dance has flourished since Maurice Béjart, a Frenchman, founded his Twentieth Century Dance Company and the Mudra school, which revolutionised dance in the country. There are more than 50 companies in residence in Brussels, most of them very contemporary. The new choreographers Anne Teresa De Keersmaeker and Wim Vandekeybus are already world famous.

CINEMAS

VO (Version originale)

Foreign films in Bruges' cinemas are always subtitled, but in Brussels you may find a dubbed version. Check the following abbreviations in the listings in daily newspapers or the English-language *Bulletin*. VO means *version originale*, subtitled; V fr, French version; V angl, English version; EA means *enfants admis*, children admitted; ENA means children not admitted.

ACTORS STUDIO

Small two-screen cinema showing five films a day, mainly art house and good films from non-European countries.

✚ E7 ✉ 16 petite rue des Bouchers/Kleine Beenhouwersstraat ☎ 512 1696 🚊 Gare Centrale/ Centraal Station

ARENBERG GALERIES

Small but delightful cinema in a converted art-deco theatre in the Galeries St Hubert, showing art house movies, and foreign almost mainstream films. An excellent place to watch some of the better films coming out of Asia and the Middle East.

✚ E7 ✉ 26 galerie de la Reine/Koninginnegalerij ☎ 512 8063 🚊 Gare Centrale/ Centraal Station

KINEPOLIS

Vast cinema complex in the Bruparck with 25 screens, the largest IMAX screen in Europe and seats for 7000. Mainstream films, mainly Hollywood stuff.

✚ D2 ✉ Bruparck (➤ 56), 1 avenue du Cinquantenaire ☎ Bookings 474 2604, French information 0900-35 241, Flemish information 0900-35 240 🚊 Heysel

MUSÉE DU CINEMA/FILMMUSEUM

Besides the permanent exhibition, five films are shown daily, two of which are silent films accompanied by piano music. This is the place to see the old cinema classics, as well as more recent films or little-known jewels from Third World countries.

✚ F7 ✉ 9 rue Baron Hortastraat ☎ 507 83 70 🕐 Daily 5:30–10:30 🚊 Gare Centrale/ Centraal Station 🚊 Tram 92, 93, 94; bus 20, 29, 38, 60, 63, 65, 66, 71, 95, 96

UGC DE BROUCKÈRE

Ten well-equipped auditoriums including the 70mm UCG Gran Eldorado showing mainly Hollywood productions.

✚ E7 ✉ 38 place De Brouckèreplein ☎ 0900-29 930 (French), 0900-29 920 (Flemish) 🚊 De Brouckère

KENNEDY

There are two cinemas here showing most of the mainstream films as well as art films on certain evenings.

✚ blll ✉ Zilverstraat 14 ☎ 33 20 70 🕐 See newspapers or display at the tourist office 🚊 All buses

LUMIÈRE

Two film screens in the Theatre De Korre building showing mainly foreign art house movies and the better Belgian productions.

✚ blll ✉ St Jacobsstraat 36 ☎ 33 88 50 🚊 All buses

SPORTS

ATHLETICS
The Brussels 20-km run, held annually on the last Sunday in May, attracts more than 20,000 runners (information **Bruxelles Promotion 1886** ☎ 511 9000). The Ivo Van Damme Memorial, one of Brussels' most important athletic events, is held in August while the Brussels Marathon is run in September.

CYCLING
Cycling is big in Belgium, not suprising in such a flat country. Most cycling races are held in the countryside. The Grand Prix Eddy Merckx, named after one of the greatest Belgian cyclists, is a race for speed cyclists held in May–June in Brussels. If you want to cycle yourself, bikes can be hired cheaply from railway stations or special agencies (► 90). The Forêt de Soignes in Brussels has very good and pleasant cycling tracks (► 57) and the ride from Bruges to Damme or to Knokke (► 21) offers splendid views.

FOOTBALL
Belgium and Holland will host the European Championships in the year 2000. All major cities have good football clubs which can easily be reached by public transport. Bruges has two football clubs in the Belgian first division, Club Brugge and Cercle Brugge. RSC Anderlecht, Belgium's most popular club, is often in European

competitions, and is an arch rival of Club Brugge.
✉ Vanden Stock stadium, 2 avenue Theo Verbeeck ☎ 522 1539 🚇 St Guidon

GOLF
There are over 60 golf courses in Belgium (information from the Fédération Royal Belge de Golf ☎ 067-22 04 40).

HORSE-RACING
There are several racetracks around Brussels and betting on horse races is becoming increasingly popular in Belgium.

Boitsfort
✉ 51 chaussée de la Hulpe
☎ 660 2839 🚋 Tram 94; bus 41

Groenendaal
✉ Sint-Jansberglaan 4, Hoeilaart
☎ 657 3820 🚌 Bus 366

Sterrebeek
✉ 43 avenue du Roy de Blicquylaan ☎ 767 5475
🚋 Tram 39; bus 30

JOGGING
In Brussels, most people jog in the Parc du Cinquantenaire/Jubelpark (► 38), the Parc de Bruxelles (► 34) or the beautiful lanes of the Parc de Woluwe (➕ avenue de Tervuerenlaan 🚋 Tram 39, 44). The Hash House Harriers (☎ 734 3677) organises fun runs on Sat afternoons or Mon evenings.

WALKING
The best place for a long walk near Brussels centre is the Fôret de Soignes/Zoniënwoud (► 57). Map available from the office.

Sports information

Two organisations provide information on sporting events in Belgium and sport activities in Brussels:

Cellule Information de l'Administration de l'Education Physique, des Sports et de la Vie en Plein Air (ADEPS) (✉ 3rd floor, 44 boulevard Léopold II ☎ 413 2837) and Sport for All (Clearinghouse, c/o Espace 27 Septembre, boulevard Léopold II ☎ 413 2893).

HOTELS

Prices

Expect to pay the following for a double room with breakfast

£   less than 3,000Bf
££   3,000–7,000Bf
£££   more than 7,000Bf

Cheap hotels

Many hotels in Brussels are business-orientated so in summer and at weekends, prices can drop by up to 50 per cent. The Belgian Tourist Reservations office on Grand'Place (☎ 513 7484 fax 513 9277) has a free list of over 800 hotels offering off-peak reductions. Although this makes it difficult to reserve far in advance, hotels are rarely full in these periods.

BRUSSELS

ALFA SABLON (££–£££)

Modern, efficient hotel with all amenities but lacking character set in an area full of antique shops.
🕀 E8 ✉ 2–8 rue de la Paille/Strostraat ☎ 513 6040 fax: 511 8141 🚋 Tram 91, 92, 93, 94

AMIGO (£££)

One of Brussels' finest hotels, perfectly located behind the Town Hall. Elegantly furnished rooms, extremely friendly staff. A favourite with ministers, opera singers and French media stars.
🕀 E7 ✉ 1–3 rue de l'Amigo/Vruntstraat ☎ 547 4747 fax: 513 5277 🚋 Tram 23, 52, 55, 56, 81 (Bourse/Beurs); bus 34, 48, 94

ASTORIA (£££)

Near the Royal Palace, the Astoria was built in the 19th century for the reception of royal visitors. This historic hotel is full of stories: the Aga Khan used to like his bath filled with fresh milk, the artist Salvator Dali gave wild press conferences and the French singer Serge Gainsbourg liked to hold court here. The palm trees, crystal chandeliers and mouldings are all still there, but mod cons have now been added as well.
🕀 F7 ✉ 103 rue Royale ☎ 227 0505 🚇 Gare Centrale

AUBERGE ST MICHEL (££)

Slightly scruffy hotel behind the grand gilded façade of the House of the Duke of Brabant. Dowdy furniture but worth putting up with in order to wake up with a view over one of Europe's most beautiful squares.
🕀 E7 ✉ 15 Grand'Place/Grote Markt ☎ 511 0956 fax: 511 4600 🚇 Gare Centrale/ Centraal Station 🚋 Tram 23, 52, 55, 56, 81 (Bourse/Beurs)

CONRAD (£££)

One of Brussels' finest modern hotels, on prestigious avenue Louise. The lobby, with huge chandeliers and marble floors, is a foretaste of the luxurious rooms.
🕀 F9 ✉ 72 avenue Louise/Louizalaan ☎ 542 4242 fax: 542 4200 🚋 Tram 93, 94

FOUQUETS (£)

Basic but adequate rooms in the perfect location for Brussels' nightlife.
🕀 E7 ✉ 6 rue de la Bourse/Beursstraat ☎ 512 0020 fax: 511 9357 🚋 Tram 23, 52, 55, 56, 81

L'AGENDA (££)

Comfortable rooms and friendly service, close to the avenue Louise for shopping.
🕀 F9 ✉ 6 rue de Florence ☎ 539 0031 fax: 539 063 🚇 Louise/Louiza 🚋 Tram 91, 92

LA LÉGENDE (£)

Attractive hotel with a courtyard and a central location.
🕀 E7 ✉ 35 rue du Lombardstraat ☎ 512 8290 fax: 512 3493 🚋 Tram 23, 52, 55, 56, 81

LE DIXSEPTIÈME (£££)
Stylish hotel in the 17th-century former residence of the Spanish ambassador, with elegant rooms and beautiful suites around a tranquil courtyard. Le 17 is unlike other hotels in Brussels.
⊞ E7 ⊠ 25 rue de la Madeleine/Magdalenastraat ☎ 502 5744 fax: 502 6424 🚇 Gare Centrale/Centraal Station

METROPOLE (£££)
Belgium's grandest hotel, the Metropole, is a Brussels institution. Built in a mixture of styles in 1895, it has an imposing lobby, while Sunday breakfast served in the Palm Court is perfect. A favourite with film and media stars.
⊞ E6 ⊠ 31 place De Brouckèreplein ☎ 217 2300 fax 218 0220 🚇 De Brouckère 🚋 Tram 23, 52, 55, 56, 81

NEW HOTEL SIRU (££)
A thirties hotel revamped in the eighties. Each room features work by a different Belgian artist. The higher you go, the better the views over the city.
⊞ F6 ⊠ 1 place Rogierplein ☎ 203 3580 fax: 203 3303 🚇 Rogier

SLEEP WELL – ESPACE DU MARAIS (£)
The former YMCA offers comfortable rooms at hostel rates.
⊞ F6 ⊠ 23 rue du Damier/Dambordstraat ☎ 218 5050 fax: 218 1313 🚇 Rogier or Botanique 🚋 Tram 91, 92, 93, 94

BRUGES

BAUHAUS (£)
Popular hostel with dormitories, triple, double and single rooms in a central location (free sheets and showers). The bar is popular with locals.
⊞ dll ⊠ Langestraat 135 ☎ 34 10 93 fax: 33 41 80 🚌 6, 16

BED & BREAKFAST MARIE-PAULE GESQUIÈRE (£)
Comfortable rooms in an ivy-clad house overlooking a park by the city walls and windmills. Excellent breakfast with eggs and Belgian chocolate. Marie-Paule's is the best place to stay in this price range. Advance booking essential. Recommended.
⊞ dll ⊠ Oostproostse 14 ☎ 33 92 46 🚌 14

CUTELINE (££)
An unusual and charming hotel outside the centre, the Cuteline is in an historic castle within the Koude Keuken nature reserve.
⊞ Off map ⊠ Zandstraat 272 ☎ 31 70 26 fax: 31 72 41 🚌 5, 15

DIE SWAENE (£££)
One of Bruges' most romantic hotels, offering beautiful rooms furnished with plenty of lace and (some) with canal views. Very central but quiet and with good attentive service. Elegant and exceptional restaurant and a delicious breakfast. Recommended.
⊞ dll ⊠ Steenhouwersdijk 1

Hotel Grand Miroir

Brussels' oldest hotel was the Grand Miroir, dating from 1286, on the rue de la Montagne/Bergstraat. Guests included Colette, Charles Baudelaire and Henri de Toulouse-Lautrec, who loved the brothels near by. The hotel gradually decayed and was eventually pulled down in the 1950s, leaving the Hotel Metropole as the only hotel in Brussels with the spirit of the Belle Epoque.

HOTELS

At home in Bruges

On holiday weekends, hotel rooms are scarce in Bruges. Many local residents therefore offer B&B, often in quiet, residential areas but, as the centre of Bruges is small, still within walking distance of the museums and sights. A brochure listing B&Bs is available from the Tourist Office (✉ Burg 11, 8000 Brugge ☎ 44 86 86 fax: 44 86 00). Advance booking recommended.

(Groenerei) ☎ 34 27 98 fax: 33 66 74 🚍 1, 6, 11, 16

DUC DE BOURGOGNE (££)

Slightly aged but comfortable rooms in the heart of Bruges, overlooking one of the most picturesque canals. The stylish, traditionally furnished restaurant serves excellent Belgian cuisine (closed Mon & Tue lunch).

✚ blll ✉ Huidenvettersplein 12 ☎ 33 20 38 fax: 34 40 37 🚍 1, 6, 11, 16

GRAND HOTEL DU SABLON (££)

Traditional, city-centre hotel with beautiful stained-glass dome in art-nouveau style over the lobby. The rear part of the hotel was an inn 400 years ago but its pleasant rooms now offer all mod cons.

✚ blll ✉ Noordzandstraat 21 ☎ 33 39 02 fax: 33 39 08 🚍 All buses

HOLIDAY INN CROWNE PLAZA (£££)

Modern de-luxe hotel, on one of Bruges' prettiest squares, built over the exposed foundations of the medieval Sint-Donaas Cathedral. Stylish, comfortable rooms, some with a lovely view of the square, and a swimming pool.

✚ blll ✉ Burg 10 ☎ 34 58 34 fax: 34 56 15 🚍 All buses

HOTEL AND PENSION IMPERIAL (£)

Comfortable rooms in a quiet street in the centre and a lobby full of antiques and big bird cages. Nice atmosphere.

✚ blll ✉ 24–28 Dweersstraat ☎ 33 90 14 fax: 34 43 06 🚍 All buses

MALLEBERG (£–££)

Comfortable hotel in old house just behind the Burg. Bathroom and TV in every room.

✚ dlll ✉ Hoogstraat 7 ☎ 34 41 11 fax: 34 67 69 🚍 All buses to the Markt

DE ORANGERIE (£££)

Elegant tastefully decorated rooms in a renovated 15th-century convent covered in ivy and overlooking one of Bruges's prettiest corners. In summer, breakfast is served on the terrace by the canal. Recommended.

✚ blll ✉ Kartuizerinnenstraat 10 ☎ 34 16 49 fax: 33 30 16 🚍 1, 6, 11, 16

RELAIS OUD HUIS AMSTERDAM (££–£££)

Charming characterful development of two 17th-century gentlemen's houses overlooking a quiet canal. The hotel is furnished with antiques and rooms are individually decorated.

✚ dlll ✉ Spiegelrei 3 ☎ 34 18 10 fax: 33 88 91 🚍 4, 8

DE TUILERIEEN (£££)

Spacious rooms in a renovated 16th-century mansion, with good views over the picturesque Dijver canal.

✚ blll ✉ 7 Dijver ☎ 34 36 91 fax: 34 04 00 🚍 1, 6, 11, 16

BRUSSELS
& BRUGES
travel facts

ARRIVING & DEPARTING

Before you go

- EU and Swiss citizens need a national identity card or passport for visits lasting up to three months. Visitors from Japan, USA, Canada, Australia, New Zealand and some other countries need a valid passport but no visa is required. All other countries need a visa.

Climate and when to go

- Belgium's climate is temperate, with warm summers and generally mild winters. Snow is rare, though December and January can be very cold and damp.
- When temperatures pick up, usually around Easter, more attractions open. In summer, café-terraces are open until late, there are open-air concerts and the sea is near by. The autumn is often rainy, but October can still be beautiful.

Arriving by air

- The international airport is Zaventem, situated 14km northeast of Brussels. Flight information is available from 7am–10pm ☎ 753 3913.
- The Airport City Express shuttle train runs between Zaventem and Brussels' main train stations every 20 minutes from 5:25am to 11:46pm. The journey takes 30 minutes.
- An hourly bus service to the Gare du Nord (35 minutes) leaves from the ground-floor level of the new terminal.
- Taxis outside the arrivals hall display a blue-and-yellow licence emblem, but are not cheap. Many take credit cards but check with the driver first.

Arriving by train

- The Eurostar train from London Waterloo arrives at the Gare du Midi in Brussels; journey time 3 hours 15 minutes, with 5 to 7 departures daily each way.
- The TGV train (*Train à Grande Vitesse*) from Paris also arrives at the Gare du Midi. There are 5 services daily.
- Direct trains connect all major European cities to Brussels, and trains from Germany and Holland also to Bruges.

Arriving by sea

- The Sally Line sea catamaran from Ramsgate to Ostend takes 90 minutes. Frequent trains connect Ostend with Brussels and Bruges.
- Ferries from Dover (UK) to Calais (France) take 75 minutes, the hovercraft 35 minutes. Frequent services. Hoverspeed offers a bus connection from Calais to Bruges and Brussels.

Arriving by bus

- Eurolines buses connect all major European cities with Brussels. The international bus station is at CCN Gare du Nord/ Noordstation ✉ 80 rue du Progrès ☎ 203 0707.

ESSENTIAL FACTS

Electricity

- 220volts AC. Plugs have two round pins. Some hotels provide adapters for appliances from other countries.

Etiquette

- If you go out with Belgians to a café, it is customary to take turns buying rounds of drinks.
- Smoking in public places is banned by law, but is allowed in

restaurants, which rarely have no-smoking sections.

- If you are invited to someone's home it is customary to take a gift of flowers or chocolates.

Insurance

- EU citizens are entitled to health care if they have an E111 form; this is obtainable from post offices in the UK before departure. It does not cover all medical costs so it is advisable to take out full health cover as well as travel insurance. Non-EU citizens should take out full health and travel insurance.

Money matters

- Belgian currency is the franc/frank, FB/Bf.
- Coins: 1, 5, 20 and 50 francs
- Notes 100, 200, 500, 1,000, 2,000, and 10,000 francs.
- Luxemburg coins have an equivalent value to the Belgian ones and are accepted.
- Larger shops, hotels and restaurants accept credit cards.
- Banks exchange money. Out of banking hours, offices operate at main railway stations, in the Gare du Midi, ⊙ 7AM–11PM, and Gare Centrale, ⊙ 8AM–9PM. Most banks will give cash advances on Eurocard/Mastercard or Visa. Several of them have offices at the airport.
- The American Express Gold Card Travel Service (✉ 2 place Louise/Louizaplein ☎ 676 2733) and the American Express Travel & Financial Services (✉ 100 boulevard du Souverain ☎ 676 2626/24-hour Customer Service 676 2121) issue traveller's cheques and deal with stolen cheques or cards.

National Holidays

- New Year's Day (1 Jan)
  Easter Monday
  Labour Day (1 May)
  Ascension Day (sixth Thursday after Easter)
  Whit Monday (seventh Monday after Easter)
  Belgian National Day (21 Jul)
  Assumption (15 Aug)
  All Saints' Day (1 Nov)
  Armistice Day (11 Nov),
  Christmas (25 Dec).
  If any of these days fall on a Sunday, the following Monday is a holiday.
- The Flemish community also has a holiday on 11 July (Battle of the Golden Spurs), while Walloons have a holiday on 27 September to mark the end of the struggle for independence .

Opening hours

- Shops are usually open from 9 to 6 or 7 (there is no official closing time). Many shops in Bruges, fewer in Brussels, close for lunch (usually 12:30–2).
  Supermarkets and some grocery stores stay open until 9PM.
  The main shopping streets and areas have late shopping one night a week, usually Friday, until 9PM.
- Banks open at 9AM and close between 3:30 and 5; some close for lunch. Offices sometimes close early on Friday afternoons.
- Post offices open from 9 to 5, although the main office stays open later.
- Museums: phone first as opening hours vary. Most open 9–4. In Brussels museums generally close on Monday, in Bruges on Tuesday. Some close for lunch, and some are open longer hours in the summer.

Places of worship

BRUSSELS

- **Roman Catholic:** St Anne's Church ✉ 10 place de la St Alliance ☎ 345 5343 ◉ Masses in English Sat 5PM, Sun 10AM and 1PM ☎ Bus 43
  St Nicholas ✉ rue au Beurre/Boterstraat ☎ 513 8022 ◉ Mass in English Sun 10AM ☎ Tram 23, 52, 55, 56, 81
- **Anglican:** Holy Trinity Church ✉ 29 rue Capitaine/Crespelstraat ☎ 511 7183 ◉ Services on Sundays at 8:30AM, 10:30AM and 7PM, Ⓜ Louise
- **Jewish:** Beth Hillel Liberal Synagogue of Brussels ✉ 96 avenue de Kersbeeklaan ☎ 332 2528 ◉ English services Fri 8PM, Sat 10:30AM ☎ Tram 18, 52; bus 54

BRUGES

St Peter's Chapel ✉ 't Keerske, Keersstraat 1 ◉ English service Sun 6PM 🚌 Bus 1, 2, 3, 4, 5, 6, 7, 8, 9, 11, 13, 15, 16, 17, 25

Student travellers

- Reductions (variable) are available on ticket prices in state-run museums for holders of recognised international student cards.

Time differences

- Belgium is on Central European Standard Time, 1 hour ahead of GMT. Daylight Savings Time (Central European Time plus 1 hour) lasts from the end of March until early October.

Toilets

- Public toilets are sometimes dirty. Toilets in bigger restaurants and cafés have attendants who should be tipped, as the tips are their wages.

Tourist offices

- Tourist and Information Office of Brussels (TIB) ✉ Town Hall, Grand'Place, Brussels ☎ 513 8940 fax: 514 4538 ◉ June–Sep Mon–Fri 9–7, Sat & Sun 9–1, 2–7; Oct–May Mon–Fri 9–6, Sat & Sun 9–1, 2–6. Maps, brochures, hotel reservation service.
- Toerisme Vlaanderen and OPT (Office for Promotion of Tourism for French-speaking Belgium) ✉ 61 rue du Marché aux Herbes/Grasmarkt, Brussels ☎ 504.0200 & 504 0300 fax: 504 0270 ◉ June–Sep Mon–Fri 9–7, Sat & Sun 9–1, 2–7; Oct–May Mon–Fri 9–6, Sat & Sun 9–1, 2–6. Information on Bruges, Flanders and French Belgium.
- Toerisme Brugge ✉ Burg 11, Bruges ☎ 44 86 86 fax: 44 86 00 ◉ Oct–Mar Mon–Fri 9:30–5, Sat, Sun & hols 9:30–1:15, 2–5:30; Apr–Sep Mon–Fri 9:30–6:30, Sat & Sun 10–12, 2–6:30.

Visitors with disabilities

- Public transport has few facilities for the disabled, but a minibus service specially equipped for wheelchairs is available at low cost from the public transport network STIB/MIVB (information ☎ 515 2365). On trains outside Brussels, a passenger accompanying a disabled passenger travels free.

Women travellers

- Belgium in general is as safe as other parts of Europe. However, downtown Brussels is becoming increasingly dangerous at night, so always take cabs and avoid walking alone at night.
- Bruges is mostly safe in the evenings.

PUBLIC TRANSPORT

Bicycles

- Bicycling in central Brussels is hazardous, but it can be a pleasant way to explore the capital's environs.

- Bruges is the perfect place to explore by bike. Outside the city, Damme is only 7km away, and Knokke or Zeebrugge less than 20km. Major railway stations sell good-value combined tickets for train journey and bike hire.

Otherwise try:
Brussels: Bike-In ✉ 18 rue Kellestraat
☎ 763 1378
Bruges: Station Brugge/Bagage
☎ 38 58 71
't Koffieboontje ✉ Hallestraat 4
☎ 33 80 27
De Ketting ✉ Gentpoortstraat 23
☎ 34 41 96

Maps

- Street names in Brussels are marked in French and Flemish. Free transport maps and timetables are available from tourist offices, the STIB/MIVB office in the Gare du Midi and the bus office at Bruges railway station.

Metro, buses and trams

- Brussels has an efficient public transport network run by the STIB/MIVB. Clean and efficient metro stations are indicated by a white letter 'M'.
Line 1A: Heysel to Hermann Debroux
1B: Bizet to Stockel.
Line 2: a circle line from Simonis to Clémenceau.
Pré-Métro: from Gare du Nord to Gare du Midi and Albert.
- Brussels also has trams and buses.
- STIB/MIVB ✉ 6th floor, 20 galerie de la Toison d'Or ☎ general information 515 2000 bus information 515 3064
- Bruges has an efficient bus network for leaving the city centre. Although this guide gives bus

numbers for every sight, the centre of the city is small and it is easy to walk everywhere. Free information line ☎ 059-56 53 53.

Taxis

- In Brussels, only use official taxis with a taxi light on the roof. Taxis are metered and can be called or flagged down. Drivers are not allowed to stop if you are less than 100m away from a taxi rank. The meter price per kilometre is doubled if you travel outside the city.
- In Bruges, taxi ranks are on the Markt (☎ 33 44 44) and at the railway station (☎ 38 46 60).

Trains between Brussels and Bruges

- Brussels has three main railway stations: Gare du Midi/Zuidstation, Gare Centrale/Centraal Station and Gare du Nord/Noordstation. Two other stations, Schuman and Quartier Léopold, serve the European institutions. Most Belgian cities are less than an hour from the capital (Brussels–Bruges about 55 minutes). Trains are good value, efficient and clean.
- Tickets are sold in the stations, and not on the train. Special offers are available at weekends and for day trips.
- Frequent trains from Brussels centre run to the outlying areas and from Bruges to the coast.
- Train information: SNCB/NMBS ☎ 02-203 2880/203 3640.

Types of tickets

- Brussels: the most economical way to travel is to buy ten tickets (*une carte de dix trajets*), five tickets or a 12-hour unlimited travel pass. A ticket is valid for one hour on bus, tram or metro, and must be electronically stamped on the bus/tram or in metro stations. A one-day Tourist Passport, available from the Tourist Information centre on Grand'Place, also includes reductions on admissions to museums.

• In Bruges an unlimited travel one-day pass is available for buses.

MEDIA & COMMUNICATIONS

Mail

• Stamps are available from post offices and vending machines. There is a fixed rate for letters under 20g to any EU country, but for non-EU countries charges depend on the weight and size of the envelope.

• Post offices usually open Mon–Fri 9–5, but times can vary. The Central Post Office (✉ 48a avenue Fosnylaan, next to the Gare du Midi in Brussels) is open 24 hours.

• Bruges post office ✉ Markt 5 ☎ 33 14 11

Newspapers and magazines

• Most European papers are on sale on publication day at city-centre newsagents and at railway stations in Brussels and Bruges.

• The English language *Bulletin*, (published Thursdays), has useful listings.

• Local papers such as the Flemish *De Morgen* and *De Standaard* and the French *Le Soir* have more complete listings.

Radio and television

• TV programmes from France, UK, Germany, Holland and Italy can be received on cable. CNN and MTV are usually available.

• BBC World Service is on 648khz, Radio 4 on 198khz and Radio 5 live on 693/909khz.

Telephones

• Some public telephone booths are coin operated, but many only accept prepaid telephone cards (20 or 105 units), available from post offices, stations, news-stands and supermarkets.

• International calls are expensive. Rates are slightly lower 8pm–8am, on Sundays and holidays.

• The international code for Belgium from the UK: 00 32. Brussels code: (0)2, followed by a seven-figure number Bruges code: (0)50, followed by a six-figure number. Use the initial 0 within Belgium but not when ringing from another country.

• Faxes can be sent from any TT (Telephone/Telegraphe) office. ✉ 17 boulevard de l'Impératrice/ Keizerinlaan, Brussels ⊙ 7AM–10PM. ✉ Markt, Bruges ☎ 050-33 36 94.

EMERGENCIES

Emergency phone numbers

• 100   Ambulance/Fire
• 101   Police
• Brussels doctors on emergency call: 02-479 1818/648 8000
• Bruges doctors on emergency call Fri 8PM–Mon 8AM: 050–81 38 99

Embassies and consulates

• Australia ✉ Guimard Center, 6–8 rue Guimardstraat ☎ 231 0500 Canada ✉ 2 ave de Tervuren/ Tervurenlaan ☎ 741 0611

• Ireland ✉ 189 rue Froissart/Froissartstraat ☎ 230 5337

• New Zealand ✉ 47–48 boulevard du Régent/Regentlaan ☎ 512 1040

• United Kingdom ✉ 85 rue d'Arlon/Aarlenstraat ☎ 287 6211/ 287 6267

• USA ✉ 25–27 boulevard du Régent/Regentlaan ☎ 508 2111

Lost property

- Report lost property immediately to the nearest police office or police headquarters. For insurance purposes always ask for a certificate of loss.
- Brussels ✉ rue du Marché au Charbon/Kolenmarkt ☎ 517 9611
- Bruges ✉ Hauwerstraat 7 ☎ 44 88 44
- Main railway Lost Property, ✉ Gare du Nord/Noordstation ☎ 224 6112.
- Lost property on the metro ✉ inside Porte de Namur metro station next to Press Shop ☎ 515 2394

Medical treatment

- Standards of medical and hospital care are high. Most doctors speak French and English. Doctors see patients at their surgeries, but some will visit if you are too sick to move. Visits must be paid for in cash or by cheque. The following hospitals provide 24-hour emergency assistance.

BRUSSELS

- Hôpital Universitaire St Luc ✉ 10 avenue d'Hippocrate/Hippocrateslaan ☎ 764 1111
- Hôpital St Pierre ✉ 322 rue Haute/Hoogstraat ☎ 535 3111
- Hôpital Universitaire des Enfants Reine Fabiola (Paediatric emergency room) ✉ 15 avenue Jean Cocq/Jacques Cocqlaan ☎ 477 3100

BRUGES

- Algemeen Ziekenhuis Sint-Jan Te Brugge ✉ Ruddershave 10 ☎ 45 21 11
- Algemeen Ziekenhuis Sint-Lucas ✉ Campus St Lucas, St Lucaslaan 29 ☎ 36 91 11

Medicines

- Pharmacies (*Pharmacie/Apotheek*)

are marked with a green cross and are open Mon–Fri 9–6. Each pharmacy displays a list of the pharmacies that are open outside these hours.

Sensible precautions

- Belgian law requires visitors to have 500BF on them at all times, as well as an identity card or passport.
- Watch out for pickpockets and bag-snatchers in the crowded areas of Brussels and around the railway stations.
- Downtown Brussels, especially the red-light area around the Gare du Nord, can be dangerous at night.
- Avoid public transport at night in Brussels by taking a taxi.

LANGUAGE

- Belgium has a long history of language division, and it is often better to speak English. If you speak French to a Flemish person, they might be offended and prefer you to speak English. If you happen to speak Flemish or Dutch to a French-speaking *Bruxellois* he will most certainly answer you in French with some disdain. It is hard to get it right and Flemish- and French-speaking people in Brussels will sometimes use English to communicate with each other.

INDEX

CityPack
Brussels & Bruges

Written by   Anthony Sattin & Sylvie Franquet
Edited, designed and produced by
              AA Publishing
Maps   © The Automobile Association 1997
Fold-out map © RV Reise- und Verkehrsverlag Munich · Stuttgart
              © Cartography: GeoData

Distributed in the United Kingdom by AA Publishing, Norfolk House, Priestley Road, Basingstoke, Hampshire, RG24 9NY.

The contents of this publication are believed correct at the time of printing. Nevertheless, the publishers cannot be held responsible for any errors or omissions or for changes in the details given in this guide or for the consequences of any reliance on the information provided by the same. Assessments of attractions, hotels, restaurants and so forth are based upon the author's own personal experience and, therefore, descriptions given in this guide necessarily contain an element of subjective opinion which may not reflect the publishers' opinion or dictate a reader's own experiences on another occasion.
We have tried to ensure accuracy in this guide, but things do change and we would be grateful if readers would advise us of any inaccuracies they may encounter.

A CIP catalogue record for this book is available from the British Library.

ISBN 0 7495 1643 7

Published by AA Publishing (a trading name of Automobile Association Developments Limited, whose registered office is Norfolk House, Priestley Road, Basingstoke, Hampshire RG24 9NY. Registered number 1878835).

Colour separation by Daylight Colour Art Pte Ltd, Singapore
Printed and bound by Dai Nippon Printing Co (Hong Kong) Ltd.

Acknowledgements
The authors would like to thank Nica and Willy Brouke-Diercx, Mr Drubble of the Bruges Tourist Office, Moeke and Leo Franquet, Pauline Owen and the Belgian Tourist Office, London, Jim Rowe and Eurostar, Irene Rossi, M. Serge Schultz of Hotel Metropole, Frank Vanderlinden and the many organisations who made our research a pleasure.
The Automobile Association would like to thank the following photographers, libraries and associations for their assistance in the preparation of this book:
Memling Museum 42b; Musée d'Art Moderne 33; Spectrum Colour Library 5a, 7, 12, 25a, 59, 87b; Groeningemuseum 45a, 45b. All remaining transparencies are held in the Association's own library (AA PHOTO LIBRARY) and were taken by Alex Kouprianoff.

Cover photographs
Main picture: Tony Stone Images; inset (a) Images Colour Library; inset (b) Zefa Pictures Ltd.

COPY EDITOR *Susie Whimster*
VERIFIER *Alison Baines* INDEXER *Auriol Griffith-Jones*

Titles in the CityPack series
● Amsterdam ● Atlanta ● Bangkok ● Barcelona ● Berlin ● Boston ● Brussels & Bruges ● Chicago ● Florence ● Hong Kong ● Istanbul ● Lisbon ● London ● Los Angeles ● Madrid ● Miami ● Montréal ● Moscow ● Munich ● New York ● Paris ● Prague ● Rome ● San Francisco ● Singapore ● Sydney ● Tokyo ● Toronto ● Venice ● Vienna ● Washington, D.C. ●